ROADS TO THE ISLES

ROADS TO THE ISLES

An Island Hoppers Guide to the Hebrides

NORMAN NEWTON

LOCHAR PUBLISHING•MOFFAT•SCOTLAND

Published by Lochar Publishing Limited,
MOFFAT DG10 9ED

British Library Cataloguing in Publication Data

Newton, Norman S. *1944–*
  Roads to the isles.
  1. Scotland.   Hebrides – Visitors' guides
  I. Title
  914. 11404859

  ISBN 0-948403-42-X

Typeset in Times Roman 11 on 12 point by Chapterhouse Limited, The Cloisters, Formby L37 3PX

Printed in Great Britain by
Billing & Sons Ltd, Worcester

Contents

Caledonian MacBrayne's newest car ferries The Lord of the Isles *and the* Isle of Mull *in Oban Bay; between them they serve six islands.*

Introduction

This book is a guide for visitors to all the twenty-three islands served by the ferry boats operated by Caledonian MacBrayne Ltd, in the Clyde Estuary and in the Western Isles of Scotland. Most of the ships currently in operation are fast, purpose-built, modern car ferries using linkspan pier facilities which allow quick and safe loading and unloading of cars and freight – a far cry from the rather primitive arrangements which existed in many places in the not too distant past.

Especially in the summer months, Caledonian MacBrayne offer a wide range of special offers, package holidays, and island-hopping tickets – perfect for the independent traveller. Known as 'Calmac' throughout the islands, the company will always do its best to accommodate individual needs. However, it is almost always essential to book well in advance for vehicles. For up-to-date information on sailing times, and to book vehicle and passenger tickets, always contact the Calmac Head Office at Gourock:

Caledonian MacBrayne Ltd, Car Ferry Reservations
The Ferry Terminal, GOUROCK, PA19 1QP
Tel: (0475) 34531, Fax (0475) 37607, Telex 779318

Ferries may be unavoidably delayed by bad weather at any time of the year, but of course especially during the winter months. Calmac do try to remedy matters as soon as possible, especially for the more remote islands, but safety always comes first. Part of the appeal of a Hebridean holiday is the *frisson* of never being absolutely sure when you will arrive and when you will leave. But one thing is for sure; after a week or two or three on a Hebridean island, there will be few visitors disappointed at the prospect of an enforced extension to their holiday.

Cars have to be checked in at ferry terminals usually thirty minutes to one hour in advance of sailing. This is to allow vehicles to be loaded efficiently and safely. Most ferry terminals have waiting rooms, toilets, coffee/soft drink

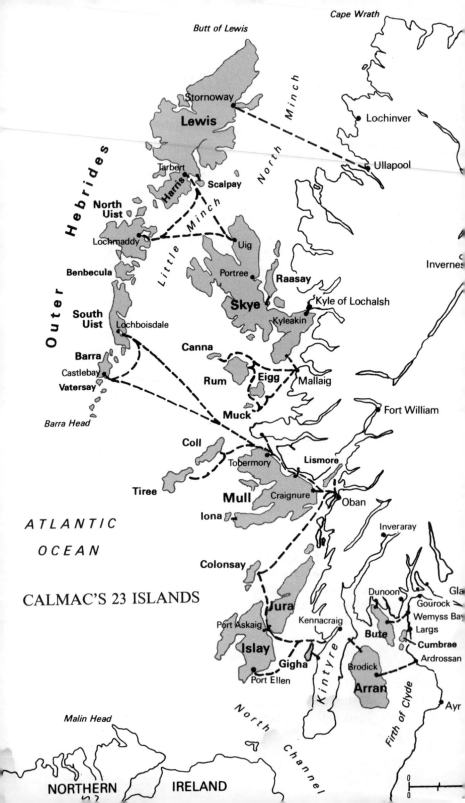

Cape Wrath

Butt of Lewis

Stornoway

Lewis

Lochinver

North

Minch

Ullapool

Tarbert

Scalpay

Harris

North
Uist

Little

Minch

Uig

Lochmaddy

Portree

Raasay

Benbecula

Skye

Kyle of Lochalsh

Kyleakin

South
Uist

Lochboisdale

Canna

Barra

Rum

Eigg

Mallaig

Castlebay

Vatersay

Muck

Fort William

Barra Head

Coll

Tobermory

Lismore

Tiree

Mull

Craignure

Oban

Iona

Inveraray

ATLANTIC

OCEAN

Colonsay

Dunoon

Gla

Gourock

Wemyss Bay

Jura

CALMAC'S 23 ISLANDS

Largs

Bute

Cumbrae

Port Askaig

Kennacraig

Ardrossan

Islay

Gigha

Brodick

Port Ellen

Arran

Ayr

Kintyre

Firth of Clyde

Malin Head

North

Channel

NORTHERN   IRELAND

Inverne

Invernes

machines and confections. However, this is not always the case, so come prepared. Nearby hotels are used to dealing with ferry passengers, and are usually able to provide teas, coffees, and simple meals in their lounge bars, as well as more potent refreshment.

Whenever possible, phone and confirm reservations. Calmac ticket offices and most of their modern ships are linked together by a computer network, which (usually) makes the process more efficient.

For the benefit of visitors, some islands are included here which do *not* have Calmac ferries connecting them to the mainland, or to other islands. There are thousands of books dealing with all aspects of Scotland's islands, so for more information than there is room for in this book, which is intended mainly to whet your appetite, please take advantage of the facilities provided by your local public library, or visit your local bookshop. Tourist Information Centres (TICs) usually sell books and leaflets relating to 'their' islands.

This book gives basic information on how to get to all twenty-three Calmac islands, and describes the main features of interest. However, come prepared to explore the islands yourself. Many people have their own special interests, and it is good advice always to enquire locally when you arrive on an island, at the Tourist Information Centre if there is one, or at your hotel or guest-house. You will find the local people prepared to be helpful when you show interest in some aspect of their surroundings. Whenever possible, buy local leaflets and pamphlets, which are inexpensive and generally excellent value. There you will find some of the details of island history, and some information on out-of-the-way nooks and crannies that there just isn't room for here. Every effort has been made to ensure that the information supplied in this book is accurate, but a certain amount of crystal ball gazing has been necessary, especially regarding ferry routes and future developments, and as your author doesn't have the gift of second sight that some of the people you will meet in the islands have, it would be sensible to confirm travel arrangements as near as possible to your date of travel, by phoning Calmac or the appropriate Tourist Information

Centre.

A word about local newspapers. There are two which attempt to cover the whole of the West Highlands and Islands, though from slightly different perspectives. The *Oban Times* inevitably is biased towards the southern isles and the Oban area, though its reports do range far and wide, largely provided by a network of contributors. Reading its columns regularly is a good way to keep up with island developments. The *West Highland Free Press* is based on the island of Skye, and maintains a more lively, aggressive and defiantly left-of-centre editorial line than its older competitors. It tends to concentrate its coverage on Skye, the Outer Isles, and the adjacent mainland, but is better at tackling national issues as they affect the islands. Started very much as an 'alternative' newspaper by a workers' collective, it is now, in its own way, very much an 'institution'.

On the island of Lewis, the *Stornoway Gazette* is still very much the traditional, somewhat old-fashioned local newspaper. But within its sometimes boring layout and typography the island pulse beats strongly. It is particularly good on local history and folklore, and has good coverage for Gaelic readers.

Many islands have their own newspapers, or newsletters, some published weekly or fortnightly, others irregularly or seasonally. The *Ileach* on Islay, published by the Islay Council of Social Services, is typical, but there are many others. The *Ileach* claims the highest saturation coverage of any community newspaper in Scotland. These organs operate as community notice boards, and as such are essential reading for visitors.

Needless to say, national newspapers are also available on the islands, although not always on the day of publication. If it is important to you to keep up with the news, it is better to phone ahead and place an order. However, the majority of island visitors seem to welcome the opportunity to 'escape' from the news for a week or two.

Seasoned island-hoppers always say that the best time to visit the islands is in the month of May. The *machair*, the lush, green, grazing pasture backing so many island beaches, becomes a blaze of colour in May and June, as the wild flowers bloom in profusion. May is also a good month for birdwatchers, and archaeologists appreciate visiting sites before the bracken and grass make identification of remains difficult. In June, the long nights guarantee extra hours of sightseeing. In the northern isles, it never really gets dark at all. July and August are the months favoured by families, and this is when island accommodation is strained to capacity and the ferries are full of holidaymakers – and their cars. It is also the time of year favoured by that rapacious devourer of tourists, the Highland midge – come prepared!

There is almost always a week of amazing, clear, sunny, dry, magical weather in September – but predicting exactly *which* week it will be is, unfortunately, an annual lottery. Those who have seen the islands in these conditions will agree that it is a chance well worth taking. From October onwards wind and rain can practically be guaranteed, but increasingly visitors are coming to the islands in the 'off' season, as the benefits become more widely known. For bird migrations, mid-October onwards is the best time of the year; for serious archaeologists, the short grass of winter makes ancient sites more visible – and more photogenic; or for those who find the islands too crowded in the summer months, the autumn or spring months are very appealing. In the dead of winter, the islands are not really a place to be outside for long, and of course in the northern isles, darkness descends in mid-afternoon in December. It is, however, a great place to be *inside* in winter, given congenial company and adequate liquid refreshment, as anybody who has ever experienced a Hebridean Hogmanay will testify, if indeed they can remember anything at all!

At any time of the year, visitors will find the locals unfailingly courteous and helpful, not to say longsuffering. Given the provocations and strange behaviours to which they are occasionally subjected, I am constantly amazed, although not really surprised, at the reserves of patience which most islanders have. There are certain basic rules which everybody should follow, and which will increase your popularity. Many island roads are single-track affairs, with marked passing places. As well as allowing approaching vehicles to pass safely, these should be used to allow *following* vehicles to overtake. If you meet a bus or a truck, you may have to reverse to the nearest passing place. Locals are often in a hurry to meet a ferry, which in many cases is their sole link with the outside world, and do not appreciate dawdling tourists. Don't get upset if a following car honks its horn and flashes its lights – it could be the island doctor on his way to an emergency.

If you should be unlucky enough to become ill while on holiday, your first point of contact with the medical services will be the local island General Practitioner (GP) or Community Nurse. Usually the hotel or guest-house where you are staying will be able to guide you to the nearest doctor. If you are on the move, camping or staying in a caravan, ask at any house, shop, post office or Tourist Information Centre. Don't forget to take medication with you on holiday if it has been prescribed for you, and tell the island doctor or nurse if you are allergic or hypersensitive to any drug. If at all possible, try to call the doctor's surgery first, or   attend only at advertised times. Most island GP's have a lot of territory to cover and a lot of visiting to do, so they are not likely to be at home if you just drop in.

Islands are places where everybody helps everybody else – it is appreciated when visitors participate in this philosophy. In the springtime, avoid fields of sheep altogether, especially at lambing time, and avoid disturbing stock at any time of the year. Leave gates as you find them – it is amazing how many people fail to obey this simple rule. If possible, avoid climbing over fences and stone walls, especially if a gate is within reasonable reach. In areas where sportsmen are shooting deer and game birds – keep clear! If in doubt, always enquire locally. Scots take seriously their rights to open access in the countryside, but on small islands these rights may conflict with crofters to whom a few lambs more or less can seriously affect their profit margin for that year, if indeed they have one at all. It never hurts to enquire politely if your presence would cause a farmer any problems, and you will almost certainly benefit from the local knowledge he is able to impart.

Always try to act with consideration for the people who live on islands, and respect their way of life. Especially in the Outer Hebrides and Skye, this means respecting the Sabbath. Don't mistake silence for unfriendliness on an island Sabbath.

A word for self-catering visitors; there is a great temptation to visit your local supermarket before your island holiday, and load up with absolutely everything you could conceivably need. But spare a thought for the local island shops. True, the prices may be a few pence higher than you are used to, but your business, and that of others like you, may in the end make the difference between survival and failure for an island family, and eventually, for an island community. Besides, island shops are a great source of news and gossip, to find out what is going on, to pick up bits and pieces of island folklore and history, to make friends who will last a lifetime. They also sell all manner of leaflets, pamphlets, maps and books which never make it as far as your friendly mainland bookstore. And they can cater for most of your shopping needs.

Island weather is, to say the least, variable. Visitors who come adequately prepared will enjoy their holiday all the more, especially those with young children. Wellies are a good idea, but are not really safe for walking off the beaten track – for that you need walking boots. Come *prepared* for rain; good rain gear and efficient anoraks mean that you can get out and about and enjoy yourself, whatever the weather. Days and days of unrelenting wind and rain *can* happen, especially in winter, but far more typical is showery, squally weather, as wind-assisted Atlantic depressions zoom overhead. Most people find those conditions invigorating, and even if you *do* get wet, the chances are you will have dried out by the time the next squall comes along! And leave your umbrella at home, unless you feel like providing the locals with a little free entertainment!

The maps provided in this book are intended for general guidance only. Serious walkers should buy the relevant Ordnance Survey 1:25,000 'Pathfinder' maps, usually available locally, especially in Tourist Information Centres (TICs). Not every island has its own TIC, but details are given of the nearest one, at the beginning of every chapter in this book.

A final word of encouragement. Many of the islands described in this book are approached from the east. In many cases, they do not therefore present their most flattering side to the approaching visitor. But after you have settled into your hotel, cottage, caravan or tent, head for the west coast, where you can usually expect to see miles and miles of empty, unspoiled beaches, and spectacular coastal scenery, where the only noises will be the calling of birds and the roaring of the Atlantic surf.

Thanks to Highlands and Islands Enterprise (HIE) and the National Trust for Scotland (NTS) for the use of photographs, those not credited are by the author, and to David Langworth for the maps of the islands.

And finally, thanks to all the islanders who helped me in my travels, and to Caledonian MacBrayne Ltd for getting me there.

Arran

Calmac ferries: Ardrossan-Brodick (all-year); passage time, 55
minutes. Claonaig (Kintyre)-Lochranza (summer only, no vehicle
reservations); passage time, 35 minutes.
Ferry information: *Booking essential* for Ardrossan-Brodick ferry;
contact Caledonian MacBrayne Ltd, The Ferry Terminal, Gourock,
Renfrewshire, PA19 1QP. Tel: (0475) 34531, Fax (0475) 37607.
Local ferry office: The Pier, Brodick. Tel: (0770) 2166.
NB: in adverse weather the ferry sometimes diverts to Gourock.

Railhead: Ardrossan – regular connections to Glasgow Central (50
minutes). From Glasgow Airport, catch the ferry train at nearby
Paisley.
Airport: none.
Island newspaper: *Arran Banner.*
Car and bicycle hire: contact Tourist Information Centre (TIC).
Accommodation: numerous hotels and guest houses, B & B houses,
plenty of caravan and camping sites.
Tourist Information Centre: Brodick, Isle of Arran, KA27 8AU. Tel:
(0770) 2140/2401. Open all year.

The island of Arran (Gaelic: 'peaked island') lies in the
Firth of Clyde, 14 miles (22km) from the mainland
coast to the east and four miles (6km) from the Kintyre
peninsula to the west, from which it is separated by
Kilbrannan Sound. It is one of the most accessible of
Scotland's islands, with five sailings daily (four on
Sundays) from the mainland ferry terminal at Ardrossan,
on the Ayrshire coast. Especially in the summer months,
booking is essential for vehicles, and even for foot
passengers on some sailings. The seasonal service from
Lochranza at the north tip of Arran to Claonaig in Kintyre
is a welcome and, in the height of the tourist season, a less
hectic alternative. Booking is not possible, but with up to
ten sailings daily, including Sundays, delays are unusual.
With a little forward planning it is possible to drive from
Claonaig over the spine of Kintyre to connect with ferry
services at Kennacraig for Islay, Jura and Colonsay, and at
Tayinloan for Gigha. Kennacraig is 63 miles (100km) from
Oban, the major ferry terminal for the Western Isles.

Occasionally, when there are south-westerly gale force

THE SOUTHERN ISLES

winds, the Brodick-Ardrossan ferry diverts to the more sheltered waters of Gourock. Buses connect the two ferry terminals.

Arran's population of just over 4000 trebles in summer. The island is 20 miles (32km) long and 10 miles (16km) wide, encircled by 56 miles (90km) of coast road, much of it on the 25 foot (7.6m) raised beach. Only two roads cross the island: the 'String Road' across the middle from Brodick to Blackwaterfoot and another road 'The Ross' across the south-east corner from Lamlash to Lagg. An excellent island bus service makes Arran ideal for walkers and climbers, and independent travellers.

Often described as a microcosm of the Scottish landscape, Arran is divided in two by the Highland Boundary Fault. The northern half is rough and mountainous. The highest hill is the granitic Goat Fell (2868ft/875m; Norse: *geit-fjall*, 'goat-mountain'), an igneous intrusion into surrounding Devonian sandstones and schists. There was an active volcano here 'only' 60 million years ago. The rugged peaks of Beinn Bhreac (2332ft/711m) and Beinn Tarsuinn (2706ft/825m) are visible over a wide area of the west of Scotland. From Islay and Jura they are seen over the top of Kintyre, while they can also be seen from tall buildings in Glasgow. The profile of the 'Sleeping Warrior' of Arran as seen from the Clyde coast is unforgettable.

The southern half of the island has a gentler landscape, reflecting the underlying geology, which is mostly New Red Sandstone, cut by igneous dykes. Glacial erratics brought from the northern mountains during the last Ice Age dot the landscape in the south.

Geologically, Arran is of great interest because of its complexity, and is a popular destination for university field trips. Recently some landowners have let it be known that they intend to levy a charge on visiting groups, and some universities have announced that they intend to take their business elsewhere! Sir Archibald Geikie, the eminent Scottish geologist, worked out the history of Arran's rocks in the late nineteenth century, while James Hutton had confirmed his theories of igneous geology there a hundred years earlier. One of the most famous sites in the history of

The long sweep of Brodick beach with Goat Fell, Arran's highest mountain, at the head of lovely Glen Rosa and Glen Sannox.

geological science, Hutton's 'Unconformity', is on the coast north of Lochranza. Here, layers of schist inclined in one direction are overlain by a layer of sandstone with a different inclination.

Much of the coastline, especially on the west side, consists of raised beaches, showing how sea level has fallen since the end of the last Ice Age. Not until after about 8000 BC did the shoreline begin to assume its current shape.

Arran's climate is often wet and frequently windy. It is advisable to come suitably prepared. Those who are bothered unduly by the likelihood of at least some rain during their holiday could think about coming in either May or September, when there are often (though not always!) long spells of crisp, clear, magical weather.

The natural history of Arran is interesting and varied. Of particular note are the seals which can be seen all around the coasts, having fortunately survived the viruses of the 1980s, and the 2000 red deer, which roam freely, mainly in the northern half of the island. There are no foxes, grey squirrels, stoats, weasels or moles. Walkers should be careful of adders, especially in rocky, bracken-covered ground. Bracken should itself be avoided in hot, dry conditions, as the spores have been shown to be carcinogenic.

The birdlife is abundant, with good seasonal variation. Most of the birds of prey which are distressingly rare now on the adjacent mainland are found, including golden eagles. Herons are common along the coasts and rivers. The basking shark, which reaches the frightening length of 50 feet (15.25m) and is seen fairly commonly in coastal waters, only eats plankton!

Arran has had a long and often turbulent history. In prehistoric times, it was settled by Neolithic farmers, who have left their traces in the fine chambered cairns at Torrylin, Clachaig, East Bennan, Monamore and the Giants' Graves (two together, near Whiting Bay). In the Bronze Age, many stone circles and standing stones were erected, notably at Machrie Moor, which must have been an important ritual centre; some of the stones may have been used as primitive astronomical observatories to track the movements of sun, moon and stars.

This is one of the most important prehistoric landscapes in Scotland underneath the moorland peat, all of which has grown since the climate deteriorated at the end of the second millenium BC, archaeologists have found traces of huts, field boundaries, and ritual sites. Some of the surviving standing stones at Machrie are truly massive, incredibly photogenic, and well worth the easy half-hour walk from the main road. There are at least six stone circles in the area, all signposted.

There is another stone circle close to the Brodick-Lamlash road, and other standing stones around Brodick and Dippen. Dun Fionn, on the headland between Brodick and Lamlash, is a fine example of an Iron Age dun. There are others at Corriecreavie and on King's Cross Point, at the south end of Lamlash Bay. Larger forts are also present, for example on the high ridge on the north side of North Glen Sannox. There is a 'vitrified' fort, with burnt stone in the rampart, on the north side of Sannox Bay. The D-shaped enclosure at Drumadoon, the headland on the north side of the bay at Blackwaterfoot, is likely to have been the *oppidum* or tribal 'capital' of Iron Age Arran.

As far as we know, the Romans never visited Arran, although their naval commanders and traders must have been familiar with it as they passed up and down the Clyde to their base at Old Kilpatrick. If the Picts ever occupied Arran, they have left no trace in either archaeology or place names, so the first inhabitants whose identity we are completely sure about were the Gaelic-speaking Scots who moved into the area soon after AD 300, as part of the territory of the kingdom of Dalriada. Probably the first Christians to come to the island were Irish monks, in the sixth century, at the same time that Columba was establishing his monastery on Iona. As both St Ninian and St Brendan are thought to have visited the neighbouring island of Bute, it is quite likely that they visited Arran too, or at least the Holy Isle in Lamlash Bay.

Arran was sacked by Vikings in 797, and was one of the islands claimed by Magnus Barelegs in 1098. Several Viking graves have been found, and there are some Norse place names. Arran did not become part of the Kingdom of Scotland until the Treaty of Perth in 1266. In 1503 it was granted by royal charter to the Hamiltons. Successive Earls of Arran played major roles on the stage of Scottish politics. During Cromwellian times the island was occupied, though the garrison was attacked and massacred at Corrie. Widespread clearances in the nineteenth century to make way for large-scale, enclosed sheep farms led to the emigration of one third of the population and effectively killed off Gaelic culture on the island.

The main town and principal ferry terminal is Brodick (pop. 1000; Norse: *breidr vik*, 'broad bay'), with many hotels and guest houses, shops, a Tourist Information Centre and an interesting and informative museum. The Isle of Arran Heritage Museum, located at the north edge of Brodick, is a model of its type, and deserves a visit. The museum is open from mid-May to mid-September. The collections and exhibitions depict the island's geology and history from earliest times up to the 1920s, including a fully-equipped smiddy, a typical island cottage, agricultural implements of all kinds, lots of old photographs, and a small research library and archive, as well as a friendly tearoom. There are poignant descriptions of the devastating effects of the Highland Clearances which affected Arran in the nineteenth century, as large-scale sheep farming replaced traditional farming communities which had existed for centuries. Gaelic life and culture on Arran was effectively destroyed, and large numbers of people moved first to the newly built coastal villages, then to North America and the Colonies. Between 1821 and 1881 the population fell from 6600 to 4750, reaching a worrying low of 3300 in 1967. Fortunately numbers increased during the 1970s, as a result of incomers in retreat from the urban rat race, stabilising in the 1980s at just over 4000.

Another essential place to visit is the Tourist Information Centre, at The Pier, Brodick. Here can be found all manner of leaflets, maps, guides, and brochures.

Brodick is a bustling, busy place in the summer season, and can become a bit overwhelming. Calmac sells over 225,000 return tickets to Brodick in the tourist season, so it is hardly surprising if it sometimes gives the impression of bursting at the seams. Yet, as on so many islands, few of this multitude seem to stray far from their hotels and guest houses, and fewer still venture more than a few yards from the nearest road. There is still plenty of empty space for the visitor to explore, and even at the busiest time of the year it is not hard to find beaches which are, by mainland standards, deserted.

At the north end of Brodick Bay is Brodick Castle with its gardens, formerly a residence of the Dukes of Hamilton but now owned by the National Trust for Scotland (NTS), which also owns the spectacular backdrop of Glen Rosa and Goat Fell. The gardens are famous for their rhododendrons, seen at their best in the month of June. A ranger service with guided walks operates during the summer season. The central Round Tower of the castle dates from the fifteenth century, but the building has been added to many times over the years, notably in the 1840s. The interior is lavishly furnished and decorated, and is open to the public. Over 60,000 visitors take advantage of this opportunity each year, making it one of the top ten most popular NTS properties in Scotland.

The island's other ferry terminal is at the north end, in

the village of Lochranza, from where a landing-craft type vessel plies to Claonaig, near Skipness, during the summer season. In the sea loch is a sixteenth century castle, overlying an earlier fortification which, together with Skipness castle, guarded the approaches to Kilbrannan Sound for the Lords of the Isles.

There are a number of settlements on the west side of Arran, of which the largest is Blackwaterfoot, close to the archaeologically rich area of Machrie Moor. Near Drumadoon Point is the King's Cave, one of the many caves where the future King Robert the Bruce is supposed to have gained encouragement from a spider in 1307. Just south of Lochranza is the small village of Catacol, with an oft-photographed row of small houses known locally as the Twelve Apostles. Their picturesque appearance disguises the fact that they were built to accommodate folk cleared from the farms in Glen Catacol to make room for sheep in the nineteenth century. A little further on is Pirnmill, where once the Glasgow steamer called on its way to Carradale and Campbeltown.

The north end of the island is attractive to climbers and hill-walkers throughout the year. There is a youth hostel in Lochranza. The climb to the summit of Goat Fell, from Brodick up Glen Rosa, is undemanding (though steep enough in places!) but ultimately very rewarding for the very fine view. On a crystal-clear day it is said that the spire of Glasgow cathedral can be seen. The tougher breed will try the jagged ridges in the north-west of the island. Detailed guides to climbs and walks on Arran are available locally.

From the south end of the island there are fine views down the Firth of Clyde over Pladda Island, with a lighthouse, to Ailsa Craig, Galloway, Northern Ireland and Kintyre. Ailsa Craig, which is ten miles (16km) out to sea from Girvan in Ayrshire, has been known to generations of Glaswegians as 'Paddy's Milestone', due to its position about halfway between Glasgow and Belfast. It is an elliptical, volcanic lump of granite 1114 feet (340m) high, and two miles in circumference, inhabited by lighthousekeepers and by about 9500 breeding pairs of gannets – five per cent of the world's population, in the

The picturesque little village of Corrie, on the sheltered north-east coast of the island of Arran.

world's second-largest gannetry (after St Kilda). The rounded, grassy top is surrounded by vertical cliffs up to 500 feet (152m) in height, of columnar basalt. The granite has a speckled bluish-grey colouring which is very distinctive; it was formerly quarried for curling stones. Glacial erratics from Ailsa Craig have been found on the coasts of Cumbria and Wales. It is a prominent landmark from most of the southern and south-eastern parts of Arran.

On the east side of Arran are the villages of Whiting Bay, a centre for arts and crafts of all kinds, and Lamlash. Details of all Arran's craft industries can be found in a special booklet, available at the Tourist Information Centre in Brodick. Lamlash is the island's administrative centre, containing the main health centre and hospital, the police station, and Arran High School, standing on the land where Donald McKelvie produced his famous seed potatoes, from 1908 to 1947. The High School was upgraded in the 1970s, and now provides secondary

education right through to university entrance level –
perhaps another factor in the population recovery in recent
years. A helicopter landing pad beside the hospital is used
for medical emergencies.

There is a monument in Lamlash, consciously evoking
the standing stones of Machrie, commemorating the
inhabitants of North Glen Sannox, who sailed from
Lamlash for Canada in 1829. The poet Robert Browning
stayed at Blairbeg, Lamlash, in 1862. The sheltered waters
of Lamlash Bay were a naval base during the Second World
War but in recent times have become a centre for water
sports; a large fish farm is a modern and controversial
intrusion, providing much needed employment at the
expense of scenic amenity beloved by tourists. Holy Island,
a mile offshore, shelters Lamlash Bay. It was an Early
Christian and medieval monastery. The cave of St Molaise,
at the base of Mullach Mor (1030ft/314m), has Viking
inscriptions. There are excursions to Holy Island from
Lamlash and Whiting Bay in the summer season. In 1263,
King Haakon of Norway anchored his fleet in Lamlash Bay
before the Battle of Largs.

The pretty village of Corrie, with its tiny harbour, lies
on the east coast north of Brodick, and is notable for its
sandstone quarries, active from the 1880s until final closure
in 1928. Some parts of Glasgow, Greenock, and Clyde
resort towns were built of Corrie red sandstone, as also
were the harbour wall at Troon and Kinloch Castle on the
island of Rum. There were smaller sandstone quarries at
Brodick, Cordon, and in Monamore Glen just west of
Lamlash. Another former extraction industry was the
mining of barytes in Glen Sannox, to the north of Corrie,
from the 1840s until 1862, when it was closed by order of
the 11th Duke of Hamilton on the grounds that it spoiled
the scenery. It was re-opened in 1919, but closed finally in
1938, when the vein was worked out. In 1934, 8693 tonnes
of barytes were produced, for use in the manufacture of
paint and in other industries. The spoil heaps of these
operations, and the remains of the processing plant, still
survive.

The main industries today are tourism, including
many small-scale craft shops, farming, fish farming, a

luxury food processing factory, and a little commercial fishing. Outside of Brodick, the island is uncrowded and unspoiled, and ideal for all manner of outdoor pursuits.

Arran is not without its problems, but is working hard to overcome them. Tourism has become the mainstay of the island's economy, which makes life difficult in the winter months. Various 'packages' can be arranged, especially for those interested in the pursuits of golf (seven courses), pony trekking, sea angling, hill-walking, sub-aqua diving, wildlife, water sports, and painting. Many small craft-based enterprises are trying hard to broaden their markets, with varying degrees of success. All hope one day to emulate the success of Arran Provisions, makers of the famous Arran Mustard, now the largest employer on the island, marketing numerous jams, jellies and preserves throughout the UK, Europe and North America. Their Factory Shop at The Old Mill, Lamlash, is hard to resist. Impossible to resist are the excellent cream teas which seem to be a feature of Arran craft shops – perhaps it is their aim to encourage visitors to take long walks in the countryside as the only effective antidote?

In recent years the extraction of sand and gravel deposits from Brodick Bay has, like the fish farm in Lamlash Bay, proved to be a controversial and potentially divisive issue. However, Arran is one place where public meetings seem always to be well attended, and they at least foster an exchange of views and, it is thought, occasionally promote mutual understanding. As in similar communities, the island has, in the end, to solve its own problems and sort out these matters among the people who live there.

The influence of incomers, and Calmac's freight charges, are other topics regularly aired in the columns of the *Arran Banner*, the island's weekly newspaper. 'White Settlers' are a problem which is likely to get worse, but the locals, and incomers who have become permanent, hard-working residents, are fighting back. All islanders have the usual love/hate relationship with Caledonian MacBrayne, the ferry company, which is apparent in all of the twenty-three islands it serves. Many advocate the Norwegian system of Road Equivalent Tariff as an alternative transport policy.

However, it is striking that in recent years islanders have become more aware of the constraints of government policy within which Calmac must work. They are appreciative of the investment in modern, roll-on-roll off ferries, and often say so, and they are rapturous in their praise for the officers and crews of the ferries – when they are not condemning them for putting their lifeline at risk through occasional industrial action! When Calmac was threatened with privatisation in 1988, and in particular with the 'hiving off' of the profitable Clyde routes (including Arran) from the rest of the company's Western Isles services, it was gratifying to notice that Arran residents were to the fore in registering their objection to the proposed changes, which were subsequently put 'on ice'.

From the jagged mountain peaks of the north to the gentle farming landscape of the south, Arran has a much more varied landscape than most of Scotland's islands, and in many ways justifies the local Tourist Board's slogan – 'Scotland in Miniature'. Administratively, Arran (along with the Cumbraes) sits somewhat uneasily as part of Cunninghame District in the enormity of Strathclyde Region. Before local government reorganisation in 1975, it was rather ridiculously part of the County of Bute. Its Highland heritage, landscape and residual culture are recognised by virtue of the fact that it is part of the area of Highlands and Islands Enterprise (HIE), formerly the Highlands and Islands Development Board (HIDB). Arran was recently described as 'a picturesque pastoral retreat on the fringe of an English-speaking industrial society'. But, although it is not as wild and untamed as some Hebridean islands, it can maintain itself as a viable and unique island community, given appropriate support from sympathetic government policies.

Bute

Calmac ferries: Wemyss Bay-Rothesay; passage time, 30 minutes.
Colintraive-Rhubodach; passage time, 5 minutes.
Ferry information: For bookings contact Caledonian MacBrayne Ltd,
The Ferry Terminal, Gourock, Renfrewshire, PA19 1QP. Tel: (0475)
34531, Fax: (0475) 37607.
Local ferry offices: Rothesay, Tel: (0700) 2707; Colintraive, Tel: (070
084) 235.
Occasional summer cruises by the paddle steamer (PS) *Waverley*, MV
Keppel, and local pleasure boats.

Railhead: Wemyss Bay – regular connections to Glasgow Central.
From Glasgow Airport, catch the ferry train at nearby Paisley.
Airport: none.
Island newspaper: *The Buteman.*
Car and bicycle hire: contact TIC, Rothesay.
Accommodation: numerous hotels and guest houses, B & B houses,
plenty of caravan and camping sites.
Tourist Information Centre: The Pier, Rothesay, Isle of Bute, PA20
9AQ. Tel: (0700) 2151, Fax: (0700) 5156. Open all year.

The island of Bute lies in the Firth of Clyde, nestled
between Arran and the Cowal district of Argyll, from
which it is separated by the Kyles of Bute. Along with
Arran, the tiny island of Inchmarnock and the Cumbraes,
it made up the former County of Bute, but since 1975 it has
been part of the district of Argyll and Bute, in Strathclyde
Region.

The island is 15 miles (24km) long and 1.5–5.5 miles
(2.4–8.8km) wide, and has a population of 7525 (1981
census), concentrated in the main town, Rothesay. The
island has a land area of 31,000 acres (12,555 hectares),
worked by no fewer than eighty-four farms, most of them
rented from the principal landowner, the Marquess of
Bute. A frequent vehicle ferry links Rothesay by a thirty
minute crossing to Wemyss Bay, on the Clyde coast, from
where a rail link allows residents to commute to Glasgow.
The modern pier at Rothesay replaces an elegant
Edwardian structure which burned down in 1962.

A smaller car ferry runs from Rhubodach at the north
end of Bute to Colintraive in Cowal (five-minute crossing).

An aerial view of the magnificent circular twelfth-century Rothesay Castle, on the Island of Bute; the sixteenth-century gateway is impressive.

At one time cattle swam across the narrows of the Kyles of Bute.

Geologically, Bute is interesting, as it sits astride the Highland Boundary Fault, marked by Loch Fad, which almost cuts the island in two. To its north are Dalradian schists, to the south Old Red Sandstone and lava flows. Bute is a low-lying island, but its northern end is more hilly, rising to 913 feet (279m) on Windy Hill.

The climate of Bute is far drier and milder, and less windy, than most of Scotland's islands. Most of the rain coming Bute's way falls on the high mountains of Arran, to the south-west.

There are several important archaeological and historical sites. The chambered cairn at Glenvoidean, on the north-west coast, was excavated during the 1960s; the pottery is in the fine museum in Rothesay. There are several standing stones on the island and stone circles at Ettrick Bay and Kingarth. The Iron Age vitrified fort of Dunagoil, on a promontory at the south end of the island, was excavated at the end of the last century and produced many interesting finds. Nearby is St Blane's chapel, dedicated to the early Christian saint and missionary born on Bute in the sixth century. The surviving ruins date from the twelfth century. The locals call themselves *Brandanes*, after the island's association with St Brendan.

The main settlement and administrative centre of Bute is Rothesay (pop. 6025 in 1981), situated on the east coast of the island, facing Toward Point in Cowal and the Clyde coast. There are shops of all kinds, banks, a post office, local authority offices, Rothesay Academy, police station, hospital, health centre, swimming pool, public library and the Bute Museum, which is an essential stop for the interested visitor. The Museum was built in 1926 by the 4th Marquess of Bute to house the Archaeological and Natural History collections in the care of the Buteshire Natural History Society. It was reorganised in 1950, and subsequently modernised. It is an outstanding example of a small, independent museum.

Rothesay is well provided with hotels and guest houses, from the refurbished 'hydropathic' Glenburn Hotel, with 137 rooms, to more humble but no less friendly bed and breakfast houses. The Duke of Rothesay is Prince Charles, the heir to the British throne. The title was bestowed on his eldest son by King Robert III of Scotland in 1398, and remains the premier Scottish title of the Heir Apparent. A Royal Charter was granted to the burgh of Rothesay in 1401.

In 1990 the refurbished Winter Garden was re-opened after a ten year closure, at a cost of 850,000. As well as housing a ninety-three seat theatre/cinema, there is an exhibition of photographs, and a Funtime Maritime Heritage Centre, which tells the story of seaside leisure on the Clyde coast. Threatened by demolition by the local council in 1982, the necessary funds were raised by a charitable trust, under the patronage of the Marchioness of Bute and Magnus Magnusson. The money was raised by numerous local fund-raising ideas, coupled with grants from various public bodies including the Historic Buildings Council, the Scottish Development Agency, the Highlands and Islands Development Board and the Scottish Tourist Board. This iron and glass building was once one of the most famous music halls in Scotland, and is a welcome addition to Bute's leisure facilities. Its successful restoration is a tribute to what a small island community

Rothesay harbour on the Isle of Bute, once a busy destination for Clyde steamers carrying day-trippers from Glasgow.

can accomplish, and also to the immense reservoir of goodwill which exists where islands are concerned.

Rothesay Pavilion, in Argyle Street, is a modern multi-purpose entertainment and conference centre, seating up to 1200, with a wide range of facilities. It is frequently used for Scottish political and trade union conferences. St Mary's Chapel, in the High Street between the hospital and the creamery, on the south edge of the town, is a thirteenth century church containing two medieval canopied wall tombs of a lady and a knight, possibly Robert II or his father, Walter the Steward. The churchyard also contains the mauseoleum of the Marquesses of Bute.

Until 1957 the 3rd Submarine Flotilla, RN, was stationed in Rothesay Bay. Its departure was a main cause of the decline in the population of Bute from 9793 in 1961 to 7733 in 1981.

Rothesay Castle is one of the finest surviving medieval castles in Scotland, dating from the late twelfth century. It has a great circular enclosing wall, surrounded by a moat. In 1230 it was beseiged and captured by Norsemen, who had to withstand molten lead and pitch poured from the battlements, and occupied again by Haakon in 1263 before the Battle of Largs. The four drum towers were added around 1300. The impressive gatehouse was completed in 1541. The castle was restored in the nineteenth century by the 3rd Marquess of Bute and placed in the guardianship of the state in 1951, though the Stuart family remain hereditary keepers. The Great Hall of the castle was refurbished in 1970. Mount Stuart, on the east coast south of Rothesay, is now the family seat.

Kames Castle is a sixteenth century tower house built on foundations as old as the fourteenth century. It housed the Bannatynes of Kames, Chamberlains to the Stewart kings when Bute was a royal demesne. The last of the line died in 1780. His nephew was the advocate who became Lord Kames in 1799, a founder member of the Bannatyne Club, which published a series of books dealing with Scottish history and literature.

Outside Rothesay, Bute is a quiet and peaceful island, with much of interest for the antiquarian or naturalist. Many interesting and informative guidebooks can be obtained from the Tourist Information Centre in Rothesay or from Bute Museum. There is plenty of outdoor entertainment on Bute. Rothesay Golf Club has an eighteen-hole golf course; there are two other smaller courses on the island, at Port Bannatyne (thirteen holes) and Kingarth (nine holes). There are two pony trekking centres, at Rothesay and at Kingarth, good fishing in Loch Fad and Loch Ascog, and two cycle hiring companies in Rothesay. There are several leaflets available locally for walkers, amateur geologists and archaeologists, and car tourists. There is a good island bus service, and also regular coach tours from Rothesay of the main features of interest. There are plenty of taxis. The north end of the island, overlooking the Kyles of Bute, is an area of outstanding natural beauty.

The island of Inchmarnock, a mile offshore from St Ninian's Bay in the south-west of the island, is owned by Ian Branson, cousin of Richard Branson of Virgin Atlantic fame. Its two farms are now unoccupied, although still worked. A rare Bronze Age crescentic jet necklace from Inchmarnock is on show in the Bute Museum. St Ninian's chapel, on Bute, is likely to be one of the earliest Christian sites in Scotland. Ninian, who died in AD 422, operated from headquarters at Whithorn, in Wigtownshire. This corner of Bute is one of its most attractive and most peaceful locations.

After many years in the doldrums, Rothesay is rejuvenating itself as a tourist resort. The annual Bute Jazz Festival in May is attracting new visitors. The Marquess of Bute supports small-scale industrial development on the island. Both Bute Fabrics, which exports 80 per cent of its high quality furnishing textiles, and Rothesay Seafoods, which produces and processes rainbow trout on fresh water Loch Fad and sea water Loch Ridden, are subsidiaries of companies belonging to him. Flexible Technology Ltd, which provides 150 jobs making printed circuits in a factory purpose-built by the HIDB (now HIE), is an example of what is possible on an island, given reasonable infrastructure, good transport links to the mainland, and initiative. Farming is still an important industry; the island is extremely fertile.

There are plans to establish yachting facilities, and in 1990 three government agencies – Argyll and Bute District Council, the Scottish Development Agency and the Highlands and Islands Development Board (now HIE) – came together to form the Bute Partnership, to promote worthwhile projects on the islands for a period of three years. Tourism in Bute grew up to serve the Glasgow working classes from late Victorian times until the 1960s. Now the market is different, but the island is adapting to changing circumstances. It deserves to be more widely known.

Loch Druidibeg Nature Reserve, South Uist, a naturalist's paradise of international importance, with a wide range of habitats.

The Lord of the Isles *at Castlebay, Barra, providing a link Lochboisdale on South Uist and Oban.*

Scalpay is renowned for its hard-working fishermen, who have modernised their fleet to stay competitive.

A thatched cottage at Sollas, North Uist, with the tidal Vallay ...nd, in an area of scattered crofts and crofting townships.

The standing stones at Callanish on the Isle of Lewis have been there for four thousand years, a Bronze Age temple of outstanding importance.

The island of Scalpay, off the coast of Harris, is reached by car ferry from Kyles Scalpay, near Tarbert, Harris.

Brochel Castle, Raasay, a ruined fifteenth century keep built by the Macleods of Lewis.

Street scene, Stornoway – a bustling town and the administrative capital of the Western Isles, the last bastion of Gaelic-speaking culture.

Loch Bracadale, Skye, on the west coast of the island not far from Dunvegan Castle, ancestral home of Clan Macleod.

The harbour at Portree, the administrative centre of the Isle of Skye, looking across to the island of Raasay.

Looking over agricultural land on Eigg to the mountains of Rum.

*The hills of the Trotternish peninsula, one of the fingers of land
separated by sea lochs, in the beautiful Isle of Skye.*

The distinctive silhouette of the volcanic landscapes of the island of Eigg as viewed from the south side of Skye.

Howlin House, Eigg, tucked into a spectacular landscape in a fragile, struggling community.

The distinctive profiles of mountainous Rum and the flat-topped escarpment of Eigg, viewed from the mainland near Arisaig.

The mountains of Rum, home to Manx shearwater and thousands of red deer, now owned by the Nature Conservancy Council for Scotland.

Cumbraes

Calmac ferries: Largs-Cumbrae Slip; passage time, 10 minutes.
Ferry information: No vehicle reservations. Frequent service; for timings contact Caledonian MacBrayne Ltd, The Ferry Terminal, Gourock, Renfrewshire, PA19 1QP. Tel: (0475) 34531, Fax: (0475) 37607.
Local ferry office: Largs. Tel: (0475) 674134.

Railhead: Largs – frequent connections to Glasgow Central. From Glasgow Airport, catch the Largs train at nearby Paisley.
Airport: none.
Car and bicycle hire: Millport.
Accommodation: hotels and guest houses in Millport, also caravan site at Kirkton.
Tourist Information Centre: Isle of Cumbrae Tourist Association, 28 Stuart Street, Millport, Isle of Cumbrae, KA28 0AJ. Tel: (0475) 530753

The Great Cumbrae and the Little Cumbrae are two small islands in the Firth of Clyde, between Bute and Largs, from where a small car ferry provides a service to the new ferry terminal at Cumbrae Slip at the north end of the Great Cumbrae. There is a frequent bus service to Millport, the only village. The main shipping channel into the Clyde passes to the west of the 'Wee Cumbrae', where there was an important lighthouse. The 'Big Cumbrae' (pop. 1600) is encircled by 12 miles (19km) of road. Once a popular resort teeming with day-trippers from Glasgow enjoying a day out 'doon the watter', it is now a quieter place.

There is a good network of footpaths around the southern half of the island, which is popular with walkers and cyclists. From the Glaid Stone, at the highest point of the island (417ft/127m) there are extensive views over the Clyde Estuary and beyond, including Ben Lomond to the north and the Paps of Jura to the west. The National Water Sports Centre is near the ferry terminal, just round Clashfarland Point from Ballochmartin Bay, where King Haakon of Norway anchored his fleet before the Battle of Largs in 1263. Other leisure facilities include a golf course, bowling club and tennis courts.

*Looking over to the jagged peaks of Arran from the island of Great
Cumbrae, in the middle of the Clyde Estuary.*

*Millport, the main town on the Great Cumbrae, has a safe harbour
and is a popular centre for water sports.*

The Episcopal collegiate church in Millport,
consecrated in 1876 as the 'Cathedral of The Isles', the
smallest cathedral in Britain, was designed by William
Butterfield in a Victorian Gothic style. Its founder was
George Frederick Boyle, later the Earl of Glasgow, who
was involved in the Oxford Movement in the 1840s. The
Millport cathedral was his attempt to rejuvenate the
Episcopal Church in Scotland. It has been described as one
of the most moving expressions of Victorian architecture
and Victorian piety anywhere. The Theology College
closed in 1885; the buildings are now used as retreat and
holiday accommodation. But it was in the local parish kirk
that, in the early nineteenth century, the Reverend James
Adam offered up regular prayers 'for the Great and Little
Cumbrae and the adjacent islands of Great Britain and
Ireland'.

Another architectural feature of Millport is 'The
Wedge', reputedly the narrowest house in Britain, with a
frontage of only 47 inches (1.2m). There is a small museum
and library in Garrison House.

From 1876 Keppel was the headquarters of the
Scottish Marine Biological Association, which moved to
Dunstaffnage, near Oban, in 1970. The buildings are now

used by the Universities of Glasgow and London. There is an interesting aquarium and museum.

The island of Little Cumbrae, separated from its larger neighbour by a half-mile channel known as 'The Tan', is uninhabited, barren, and private.

*The ruined medieval parish church of Kilchattan, Gigha, lying
between Achamore House and the Ogham Stone.*

Gigha

Calmac ferries: Tayinloan (Kintyre)-Gigha; passage time, 20 minutes.
Ferry information: for vehicle reservations contact Caledonian
MacBrayne Ltd, The Ferry Terminal, Kennacraig, Argyll. Tel: (088
073) 253, Fax: (088 073) 202.

Railhead: Glasgow – bus connections via Glasgow-Campbeltown bus
(three daily), which also calls at the Kennacraig ferry terminal (Islay
ferry).
Airport: private airfield for use of landowner and his guests.
Bicycle hire: The Post Office, Ardminish.
Accommodation: Isle of Gigha Hotel, self-catering cottages, guest-
house at Post Office, some B & B. Caravans not permitted on the
island.
Tourist Information Centre: Kintyre, Mid-Argyll and Islay Tourist
Board, The Pier, Campbeltown, Argyll. Tel: (0586) 52056.

The island of Gigha (Norse: *gja-ey*, 'cleft-island') lies
three miles west of the Kintyre peninsula (ferry from
Tayinloan). The name is pronounced gee-ah , with a hard
'g'. The locals prefer to say it is derived from *Gudey*,
meaning 'God's island'. Only six and a half miles (10.4km)
long and under two miles wide, it is fertile and productive,
supporting a population of about 180, many of whom
speak Gaelic. The only village, with the pier, post office and
island shop, is Ardminish. The parish church here has a
stained glass window commemorating Kenneth MacLeod
of Eigg, who wrote 'The Road to the Isles' and many other
songs. The old medieval parish church is at Kilchattan; in
the burial ground are intricately carved late medieval grave-
slabs. Nearby is the 'ogham stone', with an indecipherable
inscription in a script brought from Ireland in pre-
Christian times.

Following the road past Kilchattan Church towards
Ardlamey Farm and the cottage named Tigh nan
Cudainnean, it is possible to reach the south-west shore of
Gigha, with safe, sandy beaches ideal for a picnic. Offshore
here is the small island of Craro. The 'Bull of Craro' is a
rock formation, only visible from the seaward side, which
features in an island story of a local boy who was taken

Gigha post office, general store and guest-house at Ardminish, in the middle of the sheltered eastern side of the island.

prisoner by pirates. Further round the coast, at Port a'Gharaidh, is a quarry where quernstones (for grinding grain) were made from the epidiorite rock which outcrops all over the island.

South of Kilchattan is Achamore House, in private ownership, with surrounding gardens in the care of the National Trust for Scotland since 1962. The gardens and adjoining woodland, with many exotic azalea and rhododendron species, were developed by Sir James Horlick (of beverage fame), who bought the island in 1944. The whole island, including a fish farm developed in the 1980s, was sold in 1989, amid some controversy and local apprehension. There are plans to develop a private airfield and to turn Achamore House into up-market accommodation suitable for conference retreats.

The Achamore creamery, which produced a fine cheese, is now closed, and the milk produced by the island's dairy herds is transported daily to Campbeltown. The estate, fish farm and small-scale commercial fishing provide a little employment.

Despite its small size, there are many archaeological sites on Gigha: cairns, standing stones, forts and duns. There is a fine cairn at the north end (Carn Ban), and an

impressive standing stone beside the road overlooking East
Tarbert Bay. South-west of Tarbert farm are interesting
rocky outcrops carved with Early Christian symbols. The
finest fort is Dun Chibhich in the middle of the island,
reached (with permission) from Druimyeonbeg Farm. The
road to Ardailly, on the west coast of Gigha, passes close to
a small Iron Age fort, Dunan an t-Seasgain. Just past
Ardailly is another fort, Dun an Trinnse. Two stones near
Leim known as the Bodach and the Cailleach, the old man
and the old woman, are likely to be several centuries old,
but not prehistoric.

The island must have been visited by Norse raiders and
settlers during their domination of the Hebrides. A Viking
grave found by chance in 1849 at East Tarbert Bay
produced an ornate portable balance, with decorative pans
and weights, now in the Hunterian Museum at the
University of Glasgow. It probably belonged to an itinerant
Norse metalworker, dealing in gold and silver, sometime in
the eleventh century AD. The Norse king Haakon held
court in Gigha in 1263, on his way to the battle of Largs.
According to a Norse saga, his court chaplain died on
Gigha and was buried at the Cistercian abbey of Saddell,
on the east side of Kintyre. Until the nineteenth century the
island lairds were a branch of the MacNeill clan.

Gigha is an island which takes time to explore
properly. In summer the day-trippers come for a few hours
and can see a lot, but it is best to stay on the island for a
few days and search out some of the nooks and crannies of
the island's history. Unfortunately some sites are almost
inaccessible in summer due to excessive growth of bracken.
The view from Creag Bhan, the highest hill (329 ft/100m)
takes in Kintyre, Knapdale, Islay, Jura, Arran, Rathlin
Island and the coastline of Northern Ireland.

This is one island which is best explored by bicycle, or
on foot. The island's roads are all single track, and not
really equipped to deal with tourist traffic, especially in the
summer months. No part of Gigha is more than three miles
from the Post Office at Ardminish, and it is often possible
to arrange a lift with one of the locals. The local
shopkeeper, Mr Seumas MacSporran, has achieved fame
due to his many jobs, with hats to match, among which are

*Looking over towards the ferry terminal at Tayinloan in Kintyre
from near Ardminish in the island of Gigha.*

Postman, Registrar of Births, Marriages and Deaths, Auxiliary Fireman, Auxiliary Coastguard, and Special Constable. He also operates the school bus, drives the island's taxi and, with his wife, operates a guest-house.

There are four piers on Gigha, one at each end and two in the middle. At one time the ferry from West Loch Tarbert called at Gigha on its way to Islay, but now the new roll on-roll off pier at Ardminish is the only one served by Calmac. The pier at the south end is used by some of the island's fishermen.

Off the south end of Gigha are the small islands of Gigalum and Cara. The former farmhouse on Cara has been renovated recently as a holiday house. It is sometimes possible to arrange boat trips to Cara to view the medieval chapel and the 'Brownie's Chair'.

Islay

Calmac ferries: Kennacraig (Kintyre)-Port Ellen and Port Askaig; passage time, 2–2 hours 15 minutes.
Ferry information: Vehicle reservations necessary, all year round. In stormy weather ferry for Port Ellen often diverts at fairly short notice to Port Askaig, which is more sheltered. Two or three sailings/day (one only on winter Sundays). For timings contact Caledonian MacBrayne, the Ferry Terminal, Kennacraig, Argyll. Tel: (088 073) 253, Fax: (088 073) 202.
Local ferry office: The Pier, Port Ellen. Tel: (0496) 2209 (also provides information about Port Askaig sailings).

Railhead: Glasgow. Bus from Glasgow-Campbeltown calls at Kennacraig Ferry Terminal. Some buses connect with Islay ferry.
Airport: Glenegedale. Daily services to/from Glasgow Airport operated by Loganair; flight time, 35 minutes. Tel: (041) 889 1311, Fax: (041) 887 6020
Island newspaper: *The Ileach* (fortnightly).
Car and bicycle hire: contact TIC, Bowmore.
Accommodation: wide range of hotels and guest-houses all over the island, B & B houses, caravan and camping sites, hostel accommodation.
Tourist Information Centre: The Square, Bowmore (May-Sept). Tel: (049 681) 254; Kintyre, Mid-Argyll and Islay Tourist Board, The Pier, Campbeltown, Argyll (open all year). Tel: (0586) 52056.

The island of Islay (pronounced 'eye-la') lies 15 miles (24km) off the west coast of Argyll, while Northern Ireland is only 23 miles (37km) to the south, across the North Channel. It is the most southerly of the Inner Hebrides and with a land area of 246 square miles (630 sq km), one of the largest Scottish islands, covering 25 miles (40 km) from north to south and 19 miles (30 km) from west to east.

Islay's geology is complex, and includes the most southerly outcropping of Lewisian gneiss, in the southern half of the Rhinns peninsula. The gneiss of Islay is younger than that of the Outer Hebrides, but at 1600 million years old it is twice as old as Torridonian sandstone, formed from eroded gneiss 800 million years ago. Gneiss is pink or grey in colour, sparkles, and is of a striped appearance. The glitter is caused by mica or quartz crystals, while the

*Finlaggan, Islay, the palace of the medieval Lords of the Isles, the
MacDonald chieftains who ruled the Hebrides for over 300 years.*

*Kilnave Chapel in the Rhinns of Islay, where MacDonalds burned
Macleans at the battle of Traigh Gruinart in 1598.*

striped bands are caused by minerals which floated into layers as the rock cooled slowly after being subjected to tremendous heat and pressure deep down in the earth.

The gneiss of the Rhinns of Islay, and of the islands of Coll, Tiree, Iona, and a tiny part of the north end of Colonsay, was made from metamorphosed sedimentary rocks, which were originally sand or mud on an ocean floor; it is known as paragneiss, while the orthogneiss of the Outer Isles was metamorphosed from igneous rocks.

The crystalline appearance of gneiss is not dissimilar to granite. The constituents may be the same quartz, felspar, mica and hornblende. Its fresh appearance, apparently inconsistent with its great age, is explained by the fact that for almost the whole of geological time the gneiss has been buried under later rocks. The geological history of Islay is the story of how successive layers of rocks were created and eroded. In Islay it is only in the southern half of the Rhinns that the 'basement rock' – the gneiss (pronounced 'nice') – has been exposed again.

The long sinuous thrust or slide which separates the gneiss of the south end of the Rhinns from the Torridonian series of the north end can be seen on the shores of Loch Indaal just north of Bruichladdich, and weaves its way across the peninsula to emerge at Kilchiaran Bay.

Most of the higher ground on Islay is quartzite, this being the hardest rock in the island and therefore most resistant to erosion. In the quartzites of south-east Islay are intrusions now represented by epidiorite, their metamorphic equivalent.

Islay was covered by several thousand feet of ice during the last Ice Age, and there are some excellent examples of glacial landforms, notably around Loch Gorm, on the east side of the road from Bridgend to Port Ellen, and especially between Port Ellen and Leorin Farm, on the slopes of the hill there. Related to the retreat of the ice sheets and subsequent changes in sea level, are the marine-cut platforms and raised beaches, forming level areas of well-drained land. This kind of landscape is best seen on Islay around the head of Loch Indaal. Other areas where raised beaches can be seen clearly include the shores of Loch Gruinart, Lossit Bay on the west coast of the

Monument at the head of Loch Indaal, Islay, to John Francis Campbell, 'Iain Og Ile', the famous collector of Gaelic folk tales.

Rhinns, and the shores of Laggan Bay. The last post-glacial raised beach stands about 25 feet (8m) above today's strands, but there are other raised beaches at the 50 feet (15m) and 100 feet (30m) levels.

The Port Askaig boulder bed supplies evidence of an Ice Age in late pre-Cambrian times, while the broad bands of Islay limestone make the pastures of the central corridor of Islay green and fertile. In the south-east, bands of epidiorite provided the raw material for the finely carved late medieval grave-slabs which grace the island's churches.

There are some very fine areas of sand dunes on Islay, especially at Lossit Bay, where blown sand reaches a height of 220 feet (67m) and has polished the exposed gneiss. There are other dune systems on the shores of Laggan Bay, and at Machir Bay, where the sand comes inland as far as Kilchoman church and has polished Torridonian slates and grits. Probably the finest sand-dune formations are on the north-west coast of the Rhinns, at Saligo and Sanaigmore, while the dunes at Ardnave Point are also impressive. Several of these locations have yielded archaeological sites.

The natural environment is very varied, with a wide range of habitats ranging from mountainous moorland to the sheltered woodland around the head of Loch Indaal.

Ornithologists find Islay especially appealing; the rare native chough breeds there, while from early October to the end of April it plays host to large populations of migrating geese. The wintering population of barnacle geese, which come to Islay from breeding grounds in the east of Greenland, is now approaching 25,000, while up to 4000 Greenland white-fronted geese are also present. About 110 species of birds breed on Islay, and even on a short visit it should be possible to see over one hundred species.

Islay's strategic location and agricultural fertility combined to give it a rich cultural heritage. Archaeological riches range from standing stones and stone circles as at Ballinaby and Cultoon, to chambered cairns, forts, duns, and unusually, a broch at Dun Bhoraraig, near Port Askaig.

The stone circle at Cultoon, in the western peninsula of the Rhinns of Islay, was excavated in the 1970s. After several inches of peat were removed, the original Bronze Age ground surface, dating from around 1500 BC, was revealed, into which sockets were dug to accommodate standing stones. These are now marked with concrete markers. A feature of this site was that it was never completed, and all except two stones were left lying on the ground. The single tall standing stone at Ballinaby, at the north end of the Rhinns, is easily visited and is in a spectacular setting.

The quaintly named fort of Dun Nosebridge is exceptionally well preserved; its Norse name ('knaus-borg', the fort on the crag) is one of many place-names which derive from the Viking conquest and settlement of Islay from AD 800–1156. The medieval chapel and Early Christian cross at Kilnave, on the shores of Loch Gruinard, lie near the site of a clan battle fought in 1598, in the course of which some Macleans were trapped in the chapel and burned to death.

The Iona-style wheelcross at Kildalton is one of Scotland's most important Early Christian monuments. Carved from a single slab of locally obtained epidiorite, the high relief carvings are still well enough preserved, 1100 years after the cross was erected, presumably on the site of an Early Christian monastery, of which no traces now remain. The carvings depict scenes from the Bible, such as

Cain and Abel, and Abraham about to sacrifice Isaac, which illustrate the concept of sacrifice. The medieval parish church of Kildalton is nearby.

The intricately abstract carving of the fourteenth century cross at Kilchoman is also noteworthy. Several different motifs are all interconnected in carved interlacing reminiscent of knitting or macramé. There are also grave-slabs from the late mediaeval period, some depicting armed warriors and clerics. These are to be found in lesser numbers in most of Islay's graveyards.

Historically, Islay's main importance was as the administrative capital of the Lords of the Isles, the ancestors of Clan Donald. From Somerled's victories in the twelfth century until the forfeiture of the Lordship in 1493, the military and naval base at Dunivaig on the south coast and the civil headquarters on two small islands on the inland Loch Finlaggan were the centres of power for an administration which at its maximum extent in the early fifteenth century ruled all of the islands off the west coast of Scotland and almost the whole of the western seaboard from Cape Wrath to the Mull of Kintyre. Technically under the sovereignty of Norway until the Treaty of Perth in 1266, the subduing of Clan Donald and the eventual integration of its vast territories into the Kingdom of Scotland was a process which was not finally completed until after the final defeat at Culloden in 1746.

The Finlaggan Trust maintains a small visitor centre at Finlaggan, which is open from May to September. Access to the islands on Loch Finlaggan is restricted at the moment – enquire locally. Archaeological excavations by the National Museum of Scotland are currently under way at this nationally important site. Preliminary results indicate a wealth of artefacts and the remains of over thirty buildings, some of them from the period of the Lords of the Isles. There is a fine collection of sculptured medieval grave-slabs on Eilean Mor, near the ruins of a medieval chapel. The most spectacular stone is an effigy of a man in armour, dating from around 1550. The Latin inscription, part of which is now broken, translates as 'Here lies Donald, son of Patrick, son of Celestinus'.

A smaller island, Eilean na Comhairle – 'the Council

Isle' – is where the Lords of the Isles met with their advisers, and where the fourteen members of the Council of the Isles deliberated at a stone table and issued edicts, instructions and rulings affecting their territories, and administered justice.

The Lords of the Isles were descended from Somerled, son of a Celtic father and Norse mother, who drove the Norse out of the southern Hebrides after a guerrilla war culminating in a great sea battle off the coast of Islay in 1156. He was killed at Renfrew in 1164. He is often credited with inventing the West Highland galley, with a hinged rudder making it more manoeuvrable than the Viking longship, with its steering oar. The galley came to be one of the emblems of Clan Donald, named after Somerled's grandson, and often appears on grave-slabs.

Somerled's main naval base and fortress was very probably at Dunivaig, though the spectacular visible remains date from the sixteenth and early seventeenth centuries. He and his MacDonald descendants ruled from Islay for nearly 350 years, though after Norway ceded its island possessions to Scotland under the Treaty of Perth in 1266 the MacDonalds technically owed allegiance to the King of Scotland. But continual rebellions, conspiracies with Edward IV of England, and persistent threats to the security of the Scottish nation, eventually caused James IV to lose patience with his wayward subjects, and in 1493 the lands of the Lordship were forfeited, and reverted to the Scottish crown. After nearly a century in the hands of MacIain of Ardnamurchan and his descendants, Islay eventually came into the possession of the Campbells of Calder (or Cawdor) in 1614, and was bought by Daniel Campbell of Shawfield, an important Glasgow shipowner and merchant, in 1726.

Currently the population of Islay has steadied at 4000, having declined from a maximum of 15,000 in 1831. The largest town is Port Ellen (pop. 1020), with a ferry terminal, while the administrative capital of the island is Bowmore (970). These centres of population, and the villages of Port Charlotte, Portnahaven and Port Wemyss, were established by Campbell of Shawfield lairds in the eighteenth and nineteenth centuries. Other settlements include the distillery villages of Caol Ila and Bunnahabhain in the north, Bruichladdich in the Rhinns, and Laphroaig, Lagavulin and Ardbeg in the south-east; their names are a catalogue of some of the finest malt whiskies in Scotland, which constitute Islay's best known and most lucrative export. Keills and Ballygrant are small villages based originally on weaving and quarrying. Port Askaig, with a tiny resident population, is one of the busiest places on the island with ferries connecting with both the mainland at Kennacraig and with Feolin on Jura. The airport at Glenegedale has a twice daily link with Glasgow Airport; an emergency air ambulance operates as required.

Bowmore is an important centre, with banks, Tourist Information Centre, hospital, post office, police station, local government offices, Islay High School and many shops and services. There are several small hotels and guest houses. It is very much the hub of the island, largely because of its geographical location. The new swimming pool, in an old warehouse next door to Bowmore Distillery, is the result of years of fund-raising and community effort. Bowmore was founded in 1768, at which time its famous Round Church was built, replacing the old parish church at Kilarrow, at the head of Loch Indaal.

Port Charlotte (1828), in the Rhinns, is very popular with visitors. The Museum of Islay Life, housed in an old church, is well worth a visit, and has a fine reference collection of books and photographs. Across the road from the museum, it is possible to visit the creamery and see cheese being made. The Islay Field Centre provides hostel accommodation and study facilities for students interested in natural history, archaeology and geology, or for the independent traveller. There is a most welcome tea-room in Port Charlotte, which is noteworthy also for a large number of self-catering cottages and Gaelic street signs.

Port Wemyss (1833) and Portnahaven (1788), at the south end of the Rhinns, are both picturesque villages, founded by Campbell lairds. Port Ellen, the main ferry terminal for freight, was founded in 1821. Several of Islay's villages were named after ladies associated with Walter Frederick Campbell, laird of Islay from 1816 to 1848. Charlotte was his mother, while Eleanor his first wife is

Looking down towards the harbour in the picturesque former distillery village of Port Charlotte, in the Rinns of Islay.

remembered both in Port Ellen and in Port Wemyss – she was a daughter of the 8th Earl of Wemyss. Walter Frederick Campbell's son and heir was the famous Celtic scholar and folklorist John Francis Campbell, known in the islands as Iain Og Ile. Sadly his father went bankrupt and this friend of the Gael did not inherit. In 1853 Islay was sold for 451,000 to James Morrison, a London merchant banker, whose descendants still control Islay Estates.

Although having a private car is a definite advantage, there are plenty of opportunities for walkers and cyclists. The road to Bunnahabhainn is particularly scenic: to the east the scenery is dominated by the Paps of Jura, and by walking a few yards off the road the full length of the Sound of Islay can be seen, while to the north Colonsay is visible behind the Rhuvaal lighthouse, and the mountains of Mull can be seen over the raised beaches of Jura.

From Bunnahabhain it is possible to walk across open moorland to the north coast of Islay, where the main attractions are caves, raised beaches, seabird colonies, and fantastic coastal scenery. The whole of the north-east corner of Islay is a wilderness, with only occasional tracks. The south-east of the island is also wild and uninhabited, except for the narrow coastal strip from Port Ellen to

Ardtalla. The view from the summit of Beinn Bheigeir (1609ft/491m) is spectacular. The most interesting ascent is from the south-east, up the Claggain River. During the shooting season visitors are advised to check with the offices of the various sporting estates regarding access to the hills.

Islay's main industry is agriculture, with beef cattle and sheep predominating. Dairy herds sustain the creamery at Port Charlotte which makes and exports a fine cheese. Agriculture employs around 250 people on around 110 holdings. There are about 12,000 beef cattle on the island, including 7000 breeding cows and heifers. Five and a half thousand cattle are sold off the island each year as yearlings to Lowland farmers, to be fattened up before being slaughtered. There are around 35,000 breeding ewes, mostly Blackface, producing over 25,000 lambs a year. Fishing, once the mainstay of the island's economy along with farming, is carried on in a small way, mainly for the export market. Forestry is a branch of agriculture relatively new to Islay, and the spread of private forestry, for example to 3000 acres (1215 hectares) taken over near Loch Finlaggan in 1983, gives cause for concern. Tourism is a growth industry; 45,000 summer visitors come by the Caledonian MacBrayne ferries and an additional 11,000 arrive by air.

JURA

The island of Jura (Norse: *dyr-ey*, deer-island) lies to the east and north of its more fertile neighbour, Islay. It is reached by the Western Ferries car and passenger ferry from Port Askaig in Islay to Feolin at the south end of Jura (Tel: 049 684 681 for timings). Although it is not a Caledonian MacBrayne island, most visitors to Islay will spend at least half a day there, so a short description of one of Europe's wildest landscapes is not out of place.

Jura is 27 miles (43km) from north to south and five to six miles (8–10km) wide, tapering towards its northern end, which approaches to within four miles (6.4km) of the Scottish mainland. One of the last great wildernesses in the

British Isles, it is almost cut in two by Loch Tarbert. Its southern half is dominated by three rounded, conical peaks, known as the Paps of Jura since at least the end of the sixteenth century. Formed of quarzite, they owe their distinctive form to frost shattering at the end of the last ice age, which has left spectacular scree slopes on their higher levels. These mountains dominate not only their immediate environment but also form part of the seascape for many miles around. From Kintyre, Colonsay, Coll, Tiree and Mull, and from the high tops on the western seaboard of Scotland from Skye to Arran and even from the Isle of Man and Ben Lomond, they form part of the distant horizon.

The other important topographical feature associated with Jura is the renowned whirlpool of Corrievreckan – Corrie-Bhreacan, the cauldron of Breckan. This area of raging marine turbulence lies at the north tip of the island, between Jura and the uninhabited island of Scarba. It is named after a Viking who sought to prove his manhood and win an island princess by anchoring in the area for three days and three nights. Unfortunately the last of his ropes, which was supposedly woven from the hair of virgins, parted under the strain, thus casting doubt on the veracity of at least one of the contributors, and Breckan was drowned.

Scattered archaeological remains show that Jura was inhabited in prehistoric times, starting with mesolithic sites around 7000 BC. There is a single neolithic burial cairn south of Strone farm, while seven sites with standing stones attest to a bronze age population in the south-east of the island. There are several iron age forts and duns, of which the most spectacular is An Dunan on Lowlandman's Bay, to the south-east of Ardmenish.

The population of Jura has dwindled over the last 150 years from around 1000 to less than 200 today. On the other hand, the island's 5000 red deer are the main attraction for the sporting estates, which attract wealthy visitors. With only one hotel and limited bed and breakfast accommodation, tourism, apart from day visitors from Islay, is a very small-scale industry. Most of the inhabitants work in agriculture, forestry, or as estate workers. A distillery in Craighouse provides employment and produces a fine, peaty, malt whisky.

George Orwell wrote his novel *Nineteen Eighty-Four* at Barnhill, at the northern end of Jura, during the summer months from 1946 to 1949. Every summer brings its quota of literary pilgrims, who would all agree with Orwell's description of his cottage 'it's in an extremely un-getatable place'! He almost drowned in Corrievreckan, along with his son and two friends, exploring the whirlpool in a small boat.

Colonsay

Calmac ferries: Oban-Colonsay; passage time 2.5 hours. Wednesdays, summer only, Kennacraig (Kintyre)-Port Askaig (Islay)-Colonsay; passage time 4 hours from Kennacraig.
Ferry information: *Booking essential for vehicles*; for reservations contact Caledonian MacBrayne, The South Pier, Oban, Argyll. Tel: (0631) 62285, Fax: (0631) 66588. If coming from Kennacraig, contact Kennacraig Ferry Terminal; Tel: (088 073) 253.

Railhead: Oban – two to three trains/day to Glasgow.
Airport: none. Airstrip on Oronsay not in regular use.
Bicycle hire: Isle of Colonsay Hotel.
Accommodation: Isle of Colonsay Hotel, guest-house, some B & B, about 25 self-catering units. Caravans and camper vans not permitted. Camping allowed by arrangement with Lord Strathcona, Colonsay House, Isle of Colonsay, Argyll.
Tourist Information Centre: Oban & Mull Tourist Board, Bothwell House, Argyll Square, Oban, Argyll. Tel: (0631) 63122.

The island of Colonsay lies in the Inner Hebrides, 12 miles (19km) south of the Ross of Mull and nine miles (14km) west of the island of Jura. It is just over eight miles (13km) in length from north to south, with a maximum breadth of three miles (5km). Aligned NE–SW, Colonsay was called descriptively in Gaelic 'Eilean Tarsuing' – the cross-lying island. Kiloran Bay is one of the finest unspoilt beaches in the Hebrides.

From May to September there are two ways of approaching Colonsay. The normal, year-round Calmac ferry makes a round trip from Oban, three times a week. But on Wednesdays during the summer season, the Islay ferry from Kennacraig to Port Askaig continues on to Colonsay and Oban, returning to Colonsay and Kennacraig on Wednesday night. So, for the first time, it is possible to come to Colonsay as a day-tripper, spending six hours ashore, and drastically increasing the effects, and possibilities, of tourism. An influx of 300 extra visitors has become normal, adding to the 'resident' visitor population of up to 250 and the long-suffering locals, who number under 120.

The declining population lives in the three small

Patterns in the sand at Kiloran beach, Isle of Colonsay, at low tide; many claim this as the finest beach in the Hebrides.

The eighteenth century Church of Scotland at Scalasaig, Colonsay, replacing the medieval parish church at Kilchattan.

villages of Scalasaig and Upper and Lower Kilchattan, or scattered around the island in sixteen farms and crofts, stocked with 500 cattle and 7000 sheep. In 1841, Colonsay and the neighbouring island of Oronsay to the south had a population of 979.

Accommodation on Colonsay is limited, and often fully booked. The Isle of Colonsay Hotel is open March-November, with additional chalets nearby. Kiloran Estates provide self-catering accommodation, and there is a little bed and breakfast accommodation available. Caravans are not allowed.

There are some interesting geological features. The northern tip of the island is Lewisian gneiss, an ancient rock found also in the Rhinns of Islay, Coll, Tiree and Iona, as well as in most of the Outer Isles. The rest of the island is made up of rather boring Torridonian beds, but with remarkable igneous intrusions at Kiloran Bay, and around Scalasaig. At the north end of the beach at Kiloran is a fine example of a volcanic breccia, pierced by a lamprophyre dyke. The intrusion around Scalasaig is diorite, a coarse-grained igneous rock with clearly defined crystals of feldspar, mica, hornblende and augite. Contact with the Torridonian rocks can be seen on the slopes of the hill under Lord Colonsay's monument, overlooking Scalasaig pier. The low, wooded ridge running westwards from the pier, parallel to the road, is composed of diorite.

The natural history is typical of the Inner Hebrides, with the bonus of a breeding population of about forty choughs, one of the rarest British breeding birds. Buzzards are common, but all the Highland birds of prey are represented. In two or three days it is possible to see peregrine falcon, merlin, sparrowhawk, kestrel, hen harrier and buzzard. Golden eagles and sea eagles pass by from time to time but do not at present breed on Colonsay.

Colonsay is rich in archaeological and historical remains, from the standing stones at Kilchattan known as 'Fingal's Limpet Hammers' to the deserted township of Riasg Buidhe, abandoned in the 1920s. A kerb cairn incorporating a standing stone, behind the hotel at Scalasaig, is a fine example of its kind. Dun Eibhinn, also behind Scalasaig, is an iron age fort which in the Middle

A typical Hebridean farmyard scene, at Scalasaig on the island of Colonsay.

Ages was occupied by the MacDuffies or MacFies of Colonsay. They were replaced as the ruling family by MacNeills, in 1701.

There is much local history and folklore surrounding the MacDuffies, particularly Malcolm, the last chief, who was killed at Baleruminmore in 1623. Ownership of the island was disputed between Malcolm MacDuffie and Colkitto (Coll Ciotach, 'left-handed Coll'). After hiding out for several years, and avoiding capture, Malcolm was finally cornered hiding under seaweed on a skerry off the south shore of Oronsay, his position betrayed by a distracted sea bird. He was tied to the cross-marked standing stone at Baleruminmore, and shot, along with four other men. This has become a place of pilgrimage to the many surnamed McPhee, Duffy, MacFie, MacDuffie, and endless variations, who claim descent from the MacDuffies of Colonsay. The stone where Malcolm met his fate has been damaged several times over the centuries, but has now been repaired and re-erected in a protected plot.

Colkitto's son Alasdair, fourteenth in descent from Somerled, made a great name for himself in the religious

Crossing The Strand from Colonsay to Oronsay at low tide; this is the site of an oyster and mussel farm.

wars of the 1640s as a general in the army of James Graham, the Marquis of Montrose, who was trying to win Scotland for Charles I and the Royalist cause. Sir Alasdair MacDonald was eventually defeated in Kintyre in 1647 and fled to Ireland, while his followers were massacred at Dunaverty. The lands of Colonsay and Oronsay eventually came under the control of the Campbells; the 10th Earl of Argyll sold them to Malcolm McNeill, eldest son of Donald McNeill of Crear in Knapdale, in 1701.

Colonsay House sits in a pocket of mature woodland in the centre of the island. Built in 1722 by Malcolm McNeill, it was enlarged in the nineteenth century. In 1904 the estate was sold to Donald Smith, who left the small town of Forres on the Moray Firth in 1836 and made his fortune in Canada with the Hudson Bay Company. A founding director of the Canadian Pacific railway, and eventually High Commissioner for Canada in London, he was raised to the peerage in 1897 by Queen Victoria, taking the title Lord Strathcona and Mount Royal, from his Scottish estate in Glencoe and from Montreal, headquarters of the Hudson Bay Company.

ORONSAY

The island of Oronsay (Norse: *orfiris-ey*, 'ebb-tide island'), lies immediately to the south of Colonsay, in the Inner Hebrides. Islay is five and a half miles (9km) to the south, while the west coast of Jura is nine miles (14km) to the east. There are only six permanent inhabitants.

Because of salt spray, it is not recommended to take a motor vehicle over to Oronsay. Access is restricted to one and a half hours each side of low tide. In some tidal and wind conditions, the tide never goes all the way out, and wading becomes necessary. From the south end of Colonsay it takes about an hour to walk to the ruins of the Priory on Oronsay, so there is not really time to explore the island, unless one is prepared to wait for the next tide. It is sometimes possible, in good weather, to arrange in Scalasaig to be dropped off on Oronsay by boat. The Isle of Colonsay Hotel will have details.

Oronsay has Mesolithic shell mounds dating from before 4000 BC providing one of the earliest records of human settlement in Scotland, while the Iron Age fort of Dun Domhnuill is a fine example of its type, sitting on top of a classic *roche moutonée*, a glacial feature combining good natural defence with easily defended access.

Oronsay was once the site of a thriving Augustinian priory, of which the impressive ruins of the church and cloisters still survive. Founded under the patronage of the Lords of the Isles between 1330 and 1350, it was the location of one of the workshops in the West Highlands which produced intricately carved grave-slabs and stone crosses until 1500. The Oronsay Cross is a fine example.

Mull

Calmac ferries: Oban-Craignure; passage time, 40 minutes. Oban-Tobermory; passage time 1 hour 45 minutes. Lochaline-Fishnish; passage time, 15 minutes. Kilchoan (Ardnamurchan)-Tobermory (summer only); passage time, 35 minutes. Summer Sundays Mallaig-Armadale-Tobermory-Coll-Tiree round trip.
Ferry information: For vehicle reservations contact Caledonian MacBrayne Ltd, The South Pier, Oban, Argyll. Tel: (0631) 62285, Fax: (0631) 66588.
The ferry from Oban-Coll/Tiree calls at Tobermory on most sailings. Local ferry offices: Craignure, Tel: (068 02) 343; Tobermory, (0688) 2017.

Railhead: Oban.
Airport: private airstrip at Glenforsa.
Car and bicycle hire: Craignure, Tobermory.
Island newspaper: *Am Muileach.*
Accommodation: Hotels, guest-houses, B & B, self-catering, caravans, camping.
Tourist Information Centre: Tobermory, Tel: (0688) 2182. Oban, Mull & District Tourist Board, Bothwell House, Argyll Square, Oban, Argyll. Tel: (0631) 63122.

The island of Mull lies off the coast of Argyll, forming the western entrance to the Firth of Lorn and Loch Linnhe. To its north, across the narrow, fjordlike Sound of Mull, lies Morvern and the Ardnamurchan peninsula. To the south are Colonsay, Islay and Jura, while to the west are Coll, Tiree, Iona, and the waters of the North Atlantic. With a land area of 353 square miles (904sq km), its population of just under 2400 is scattered thinly but unevenly across the landscape, with the largest settlements at Tobermory (700), Craignure, Salen, Bunessan, Dervaig and Fionnphort.

A feature of the topography is the way in which sea lochs bite into the middle of the island. Loch na Keal, Loch Scridain, Loch Buie and Loch Spelve all provide sheltered anchorages. There are 300 miles (480km) of coastline.

Mull is well served by ferry services. The main connection is from the railhead at Oban to Craignure, at the eastern entrance of the Sound of Mull; this is a forty-minute crossing. A shorter voyage across the Sound of Mull from Lochaline to Fishnish gives access from Morvern, Lochaber and Fort William. In addition, ferries heading for Coll and Tiree call at Tobermory. A summer service links Kilchoan (Ardnamurchan) with Tobermory.

Mull is a picturesque and hilly island, dominated by the central mountain of Ben More (3170ft/967m), from which there is a spectacular view. Its scree slopes are the remains of an ancient volcano which exploded 60 million years ago. All around the central plateau are basaltic lavas, forming gigantic terraced steps. The interesting geology attracts many students and field workers during the summer months. Near the headland of the Ardmeanach peninsula is MacCulloch's Tree, a remarkable geological fossil tree discovered in 1819. Today only the base of the trunk survives, consisting of a partially silicified cylinder of fossil wood glistening with quartz crystals, surrounded by a sheath of soft, black, charred wood. It is rooted in a carbonaceous mud with a film of coal, overlying a bed of red volcanic ash.

There are many sites of archaeological and historical interest, ranging from chambered cairns and standing stones to vitrified forts, duns and brochs, and several important castles. The stone circle at the head of Loch Buie, and the linear settings of standing stones in the forestry plantations around Dervaig, are evidence of ceremonial observances in Mull in the bronze age, dating to the second millennium BC. The Iron Age Dun Aisgain, near Burg, is exceptionally well-preserved, dating as it does from around 200 BC.

Duart Castle, near Craignure, was probably built as a MacDougall castle in the thirteenth century. The main feature is the tower house built in the late fourteeth century, when it became the chief residence of the MacLeans of Duart. The MacLeans lost their estates in the 1670s, but in 1911 Duart Castle was purchased and restored by Colonel Sir Fitzroy MacLean, 26th Chief of the clan MacLean. It is now a place of pilgrimage for the Maclean diaspora.

Aros Castle, on the Sound of Mull near Salen, dates from the fourteenth century and was one of the

strongholds of the Lords of the Isles. Moy Castle, at the
head of Loch Buie, was built in the fifteenth century by the
MacLeans of Lochbuie. The strangely-named Frank
Lockwood's Island, east of the entrance to Loch Buie,
recalls the Solicitor-General in Lord Rosebery's administration, 1894-5. He was the brother-in-law of the 21st
MacLaine (sic) of Lochbuie.

Torosay Castle, to the south of Craignure, was built in
1856 in the Scottish baronial style. There are fine gardens,
through which runs a narrow-gauge railway which has
become a major tourist attraction. Another modern castle
is Glengorm, on the Mishnish promontory west of
Tobermory; it was built in 1860.

The long, low peninsula of the Ross of Mull is
traversed by an ancient pilgrim track, aiming for the island
of Iona lying at its western extremity. The modern road
system of Mull amounts to over 120 miles (192km), much
of it greatly improved in recent years. Close to the south-
west tip of the Ross of Mull is the island of Erraid,
immortalised by Robert Louis Stevenson in *Kidnapped*. It
was here that David Balfour was shipwrecked from the brig
Covenant, and began his adventures. The cottages were
built as a shore station by the Commissioners of Northern
Lights for keepers serving the lighthouses at Skerryvore
and Dubh Artach. The engineer on these projects, and
others, was Alan Stevenson, uncle of the writer. The island
is now occupied by members of the Findhorn Foundation.

As well as being one of the smallest Scottish burghs,
Tobermory is also one of the most colourful; brightly
painted houses line the sheltered harbour. The town was
built in 1787-8 by the British Fisheries Society. An annual
music festival and yacht races are among the major events
held there. There are many hotels and guest-houses, and a
youth hostel, providing accommodation. As befits the
island's 'capital', there is a good range of shops and
facilities, including a Tourist Information Centre.

The population of Mull grew dramatically in the
eighteenth century, and peaked at 10,600 in 1821, but has
been declining ever since. In recent years numbers have
stabilised around 2300-2400, although the replacement of
native islanders by both English and Scottish incomers is

A peaceful scene at Bunessan, Mull, at the head of Loch na Lathaich in the Ross of Mull.

more apparent, and thus has aroused more controversy, on Mull than on the many other Hebridean islands with which it shares this trend. The locals refer to the incomers as 'White Settlers', and sometimes refer to the island as 'The Officers' Mess'. During the summer the resident population rises to over 8000.

The lack of adequate medical facilities for the population is an ongoing subject of controversy, as on many other islands. Often elderly patients have to be sent to the mainland, to hospitals in Oban or Glasgow, from which they may never return, causing great distress to relatives. At Dunaros Hospital, Salen, there are only five beds, and the local GPs provide emergency cover. Ambulances are often seen on the Craignure-Oban ferry, taking patients over for treatment, or to the maternity hospital there. In 1990 Calmac delayed one of their sailings for thirty minutes for an expectant mother, precipitating lengthy correspondence in the *Oban Times* when a bus courier wrote in complaining bitterly because his paying customers were late for dinner at their Oban hotel. Not all visitors are so insensitive.

Dervaig is home to the thirty-five-seat Mull Little Theatre, founded in 1966 by Barrie and Marianne Hesketh

A panoramic view of reflections on the harbour at Tobermory, Mull – one of several areas of sheltered woodland on the Sound of Mull.

and run by them until 1984. Their successors are carrying on the tradition of providing high quality dramatic entertainment in what was a disused cow byre. It is Britain's smallest professional theatre. As their publicity material says, if you draw a line from Inverness to Glasgow the only theatre between you and Broadway is the Little Theatre, Mull.

In modern times, the Forestry Commission, small-scale crofting and fishing, sheep farming, fish farming and tourism (over 600,000 annual visitors) are the major industries on Mull.

The island of Ulva (Norse 'wolf island') lies in Loch Tuath, off the west coast of Mull, now connected by a bridge to the neighbouring island of Gometra. The population of over 500 was completely cleared between 1846 and 1851. Owned by MacQuarries for over 800 years, it was the birthplace of the father of Major-General Lachlan MacQuarie (*sic*), Governor-General of New South Wales, an important figure in Australian colonial history. The grandfather of the famous missionary and explorer David Livingstone was a crofter in Ulva.

From Ulva Ferry it is possible to arrange boat trips to the offshore island of Staffa. This tiny island consists of 71

*Essential elements of Hebridean life at Bunessan, Mull, on the
ancient pilgrim route to Iona: lobster creels, hotel and kirk.*

acres (29 hectares) of columnar basalt. The hexagonal
columns result from the slow cooling of Tertiary basalt
lavas, 60 million years ago. Geologically they are similar to
the Giant's Causeway in Antrim and to formations on the
Ardmeanach peninsula on Mull, six miles (10km) to the
south-east. Landing is possible only in calm sea conditions.
Boat trips to Staffa visit the musical cave, An Uamh Binn,
in which the sound of the sea amongst the columns made
such an impression on Felix Mendelssohn in 1829. The
island is immortalised in his *Hebrides Overture*.

Iona

Calmac ferries: Fionnphort (Mull)-Iona; passage time, 5 minutes.
Ferry information: Vehicles not usually carried. Frequent sailings. In summer, excursions from Oban are available, allowing two hours ashore at Iona.

Railhead: Oban. Calmac ferry Oban-Craignure, local bus.
Airport: none.
Accommodation: Hotels, guest-houses, B & B, hostel at Abbey.
Tourist Information Centre: Oban, Mull & District Tourist Board, Bothwell House, Argyll Square, Oban, Argyll. Tel: (0631) 63122.

Iona is a small island, barely 3.5 by 1.5 miles (5.6 by 2.4km) overall, with historical importance out of all proportion to its size. It lies just off the end of the Ross of Mull – the long peninsula at the south-west corner of Mull along which a pilgrim's way leads to the holy island of Iona.

The place-name, according to the latest scholarship emanating from the Royal Commission on the Ancient and Historical Monuments of Scotland (RCAHMS), is from a misreading of the Latin *Ioua insula*, meaning something like 'yewy island', from the ancient Irish *iwos*, 'yew tree'. They point out that the reason the mistake gained acceptance was that the word *Iona* (*Jonah*) is the Hebrew equivalent of the Latin *Columba*, 'a dove', which was the church name of Colum, the Irish monk who came here with his companions in AD 563. St Columba is known in Gaelic as *Colum Cille*, which explains the Gaelic name for the island, *I Chaluim Chille*.

Although there are one or two prehistoric sites on the island, notably the Iron Age fort on the summit of Dun Cul Bhuirg, Iona owes all of its known history to one man, the Early Christian saint and missionary, St Columba, who founded a monastery there in AD 563. It was typical of the small offshore islands apparently irresistable to early Celtic christians. The first religious community on Iona would have consisted of a few monks living in separate huts, grouped around a small church – quite unlike the great monasteries of the Middle Ages. Apart from the

A general view of St Mary's Abbey, Iona, an Augustinian monastery dating from the thirteenth century.

elaborately carved stone crosses and the earthen bank which surrounded their foundation, few traces now remain. The impressive medieval church and monastic complex, viewed annually by over 600,000 tourists, was founded around 1200 as a Benedictine abbey by Reginald, son of Somerled who freed the southern isles from Norse rule.

After the forfeiture of the MacDonald Lords of the Isles in 1493 the Abbey lost its independent status, and after the Protestant Reformation in the 1560s it fell into disrepair. The ruins were gifted by the 8th Duke of Argyll to the Iona Cathedral Trust in 1899, on condition that they re-roof the medieval church and restore it for worship. This was accomplished by 1910. In 1938 Dr George MacLeod (now the Very Reverend Lord MacLeod of Fuinary) founded the Iona Community as an evangelical Church of Scotland brotherhood, with the abbey buildings as its headquarters. This body organised working parties, and by 1965 had succeeded in restoring the other monastic buildings in the abbey complex. In 1979 the island of Iona (except for the abbey buildings) was sold by the Trustees of the 10th Duke of Argyll to the Fraser Foundation, who then presented it to the Scottish nation in memory of the

St Martin's Cross, Iona; an eighth-century AD Early Christian cross near the site of the monastery founded by St Columba in AD 563.

late Lord Fraser of Allander. Subsequently the Secretary of State for Scotland transferred ownership to the National Trust for Scotland.

Several guides to Iona Abbey are sold locally, of which by far the best is that prepared for the RCAHMS. The abbey bookshop is well stocked with books on Scottish history, and sells a range of souvenirs. The abbey Museum, in what was probably the monastic infirmary, houses the restored St John's Cross, and assorted architectural fragments. There are also a large number of Early Christian cross-marked stones displayed there.

The oldest part of the abbey is the small, steep-roofed building tucked away in a corner just north of the main west door of the abbey church. Although much restored (only the footings of the original structure survive), this is likely to be an oratory of ninth or tenth century date, and almost certainly marks the site of St Columba's tomb.

The small building south-west of the abbey is St Oran's Chapel, probably built as a family mortuary chapel by Somerled, the ruler of the Isles (d. 1164) or his son Reginald. Surrounding it is the *Reilig Odhrain*, 'the burial-ground of Oran', which reputedly contains the burials of 48 Scottish kings, including Macbeth's victim, Duncan.

*The 8th Duke of Argyll and his third wife Duchess Ina lie together in
Carrara marble effigies in Iona Abbey.*

There are also supposed to be four Irish and eight
Norwegian kings buried here. The stone slabs in the ground
are not the graves of these kings, but mark the last resting
place of various important people from around the West
Highland and Islands who were buried at Iona in the late
Middle Ages and later.

Without a doubt the most important Christian monuments on Iona are the Early Christian High Crosses. They
date from the beginning of the eighth century. The most
spectacular, and most often reproduced are St Martin's
Cross, which has a small 'wheel', and St John's Cross. It is
a replica of St John's Cross which stands in front of the
abbey; the restored original is in the Abbey Museum. The
east face of St Martin's Cross shows the Virgin and Child,
Daniel in the Lions' Den and Abraham's sacrifice of Isaac.

An Augustinian nunnery, founded about 1200, stands
just outside the village. Between it and Iona Abbey is
MacLean's Cross, a late medieval intricately carved cross,
with a crucifix on the west face.

Geologically Iona is quite different from Mull.
Whereas Mull is basically a volcanic landscape, Iona has
more in common with the Outer Hebrides, at least as far as
its rocks are concerned. Some of it is made up of

Torridonian sandstone, but the basement rock is Lewisian
gneiss. In many ways it is geologically very similar to the
Rhinns of Islay. Iona marble was formerly quarried on the
south-east corner of the island at *Rubha na carraig geire*,
'the point of the sharp rock'. Early records show quarrying
on Iona in 1693, but the rusting machinery, gunpowder
store and rough quay date from 1907–14. Polished pebbles
of the yellowish-green serpentine stone can be picked up on
most of Iona's beaches.

Today's resident population numbers about 100,
excluding the temporary visitors staying in the accommodation blocks at the Abbey. Obviously the island is
swamped in the summer months by day trippers, but it is
astonishing how few of them venture more than a few
yards from the paved roads, leaving the rest of the island
relatively unspoiled. But visitors should remember that the
local people are going about their daily lives, and show
appropriate consideration. In 1990 a new visitor centre
opened, in the old manse, with exhibits and displays illustrating the daily life of the working people of the island
from 1770 to the present day. Old photographs show the
traditional activities of crofting, fishing, schooling, and the
coming of the steamboats from Oban that began the tourist
boom.

Many visitors come to Iona as a genuine pilgrimage,
and it is only the totally insensitive who fail to be moved by
the spiritual qualities of the place, despite the tourist
hordes. One of the first tourists to Iona was Dr Samuel
Johnson, who spoke eloquently about the island on behalf
of the millions who have followed in his footsteps:

> *We were now treading that illustrious island, which*
> *was once the luminary of the Caledonian regions,*
> *whence savage clans and roving barbarians derived the*
> *benefits of knowledge, and the blessings of religion.*
> *To abstract the mind from all local emotion would be*
> *impossible if it were endeavoured, and would be*
> *foolish if it were possible. Whatever withdraws us*
> *from the power from our senses, whatever makes the*
> *past, the distant, or the future, predominate over the*
> *present, advances us in the dignity of thinking*

being.... That man is little to be envied whose patriotism would not gain force upon the field of Marathon *or whose piety would not grow warmer among the ruins of* Iona*!*

Although undoubtedly genuinely moved by the place and its history, both Dr Johnson and his companion, James Boswell, were disappointed with what they saw at Iona. Having heard that kings of Scotland were buried there, they apparently expected something more grand, along the lines of Westminster Abbey!

Lismore

Calmac ferries: Oban-Lismore (Achnacroish); passage time, 50 minutes.
Ferry information: For vehicle reservations contact Caledonian MacBrayne Ltd, The South Pier, Oban, Argyll. Tel: (0631) 62285, Fax: (0631) 66588.
There is also a passenger ferry from Port Appin on the mainland to Point at the north end of Lismore; passage time, 10 minutes.

Railhead: Oban.
Airport: none.
Accommodation: Guest-house, self-catering cottages, B & B.
Tourist Information Centre: Oban, Mull % District Tourist Board, Bothwell House, Argyll Square, Oban, Argyll. Tel: (0631) 63122.

The fertile island of Lismore (Gaelic: *leis mor*, 'the big garden'), lies in Loch Linnhe, one to two miles (1.6–3.2km) off the coasts of Benderloch and Appin on the Scottish mainland. The population is about 140. The ferry terminal is at Achnacroish, half way up the eastern side of the island. Most of the houses and farms are concentrated in the low-lying and more fertile northern half of Lismore. Until the end of the sixteenth century the island was covered by oak woods, which were cut down for charcoal to fuel Lorn's iron furnaces, for shipbuilding, and to clear the hills for cattle and sheep.

The fertility and productiveness of Lismore is due to the ridges of Dalradian limestone which make up most of the island. Limestone was quarried formerly at An Sailean on the west coast, and exported to the mainland from Port Ramsay. There are fine raised beaches around the shoreline, reflecting changes in sea level at the end of the last Ice Age. The highest point of the island is Barr Mor (416ft/127m).

A single road runs down the centre of the island, ending in a track leading to the south point, opposite Eilean Musdile, where there is a lighthouse built in 1833, now automatic. Lismore is just under ten miles (16km) long

On the Lismore skyline, the Iron Age broch tower of Tirefour, an
important island fortress in prehistoric times.

and 1.5 miles (2.4km) wide, with a land area of 10,000
acres. The island has a long and interesting history. In
prehistoric times a broch tower was built at Tirefour, about
1.5 miles (2.4km) south of Point or 2.5 miles (4km) north
of Achnacroish pier. Although ruinous, many typical
broch features survive, including the concentric dry-stone
walls and mural galleries, and it is in fact regarded as one
of the best-preserved prehistoric monuments in Argyll. On
the south-east side it survives to a height of nearly 16 feet
(5m). The walls have been quarried for building stone, but
the site has never been excavated.

For several centuries in the Middle Ages, Lismore was
the ecclesiastical capital of Argyll. A cathedral for the new
diocese of Argyll was founded around 1189, and dedicated
to St Moluag. It continued in use until the sixteenth
century. Several interesting medieval architectural features
survive, including the north choir doorway, and a piscina,
sedilia and doorway in the south choir wall. The choir of
the medieval cathedral is now used as the parish church, as
the result of renovations carried out about 1900. The
cathedral probably occupies the site of a church founded
by the Irish saint Moluag (Lugaidh), who founded a
religious community on Lismore in the second half of the

sixth century, at about the same time St Columba was establishing his monastery in Iona, in 563. Local tradition holds that the wooden staff, the *Bachuil Mor*, which can be seen in Bachuil House, belonged to St Moluag. A bell and bell shrine which are believed to have belonged to the saint are in the Royal Museum of Scotland, in Edinburgh.

A rather gory tradition relating to St Columba and St Moluag has it that the two saints were racing to see who could set foot first on Lismore, to establish a monastery there. As St Columba's coracle forged ahead, Moluag cut off a finger and threw it on to the island, thus claiming first possession. Similar stories abound in Celtic folklore and should not be taken too literally.

In the south-west of the island, near the shore, is the thirteenth century Achadun Castle, built for the bishops of Argyll. It fell into ruins after Bishop David Hamilton had a new castle built at Saddell, in Kintyre, in 1508. It is reached by taking the road to Achanduin farm, and following a track from there. From the castle it is a short walk to Bernera Island, which can be reached at low tide. Visitors should take care not to get themselves stranded! There is a tradition that St Columba preached under a great yew tree on Bernera Island, and in the stained glass window in the east gable of the parish church of Lismore he is shown blessing this tree.

On the west coast of Lismore, opposite the cathedral of St Moluag, is Castle Coeffin, a thirteenth century hall-house and bailey. It was probably erected by one of the MacDougalls of Lorn, for the island of Lismore occupied an important strategic position within their territories. According to local legend, the unusual name comes from the legendary Norse Prince Caifean. In 1470 it was acquired by the Campbells of Glenorchy, and remained in their hands until the early eighteenth century.

Lismore makes an interesting destination for a day trip. It is ideal for walkers and cyclists, although it has to be said that the rainfall is double that of the east of Scotland. There are spectacular views up and down Loch Linnhe, taking in the Paps of Jura to the south, the mountains of Mull and Morvern, Ben Nevis to the north, and Cruachan to the east. Accommodation on the island is limited, and booking is required. The guesthouse beside St Moluag's cathedral provides teas, coffees, lunches and dinners. There is a small general store and post office situated at Clachan, a mile south of the church. Visitors coming to stay on the island are advised to order bread, milk and newspapers well in advance.

Coll

Calmac ferries: Oban-Tobermory-Coll; passage time, 3 hours. Tiree-Coll; passage time, 1. hour 15 minutes. Tobermory-Coll; passage time, 1. hour 15 minutes. Sailing days vary seasonally, but are three times/week in winter, four times/week in summer. Summer Sundays: Mallaig-Armadale-Tobermory-Coll-Tiree round trip.

Ferry information: For vehicle reservations contact Caledonian MacBrayne Ltd, The South Pier, Oban, Argyll. Tel: (0631) 62285, Fax; (0631) 66588. Most ferries leave Oban at 6.00 am. Overnight berths bookable on ferry.

At present vehicles are unloaded by means of a side lift, but new roll-on, roll-off facilities are planned in the near future.

Local ferry office: The Pier, Arinagour, Isle of Coll, Argyll. Tel: (087 93) 347.

Railhead: Oban.

Airport: none. There is a private airstrip at Breachacha, and an airport on Tiree.

Accommodation: Isle of Coll Hotel, guest-house, self-catering cottages, some B & B.

Tourist Information Centre: Oban, Mull & District Tourist Board, Bothwell House, Argyll Square, Oban, Argyll. Tel: (0631) 63122.

The island of Coll lies in the Inner Hebrides, north-west of the island of Mull. The population is about 150. A car ferry from Oban calls at the main township, Arinagour, before continuing to the neighbouring island of Tiree. In size the island measures 13 miles (21km) by four miles (6.4km); the terrain is generally low-lying but knobbly, due to the underlying Lewisian gneiss, especially in the northern half of the island. A thin vein of lead at Crossapol was once mined. Garnets are found on the shore south-west of Breachacha. The highest hill is Ben Hogh (341 ft/104m), on top of which a large glacial erratic is precariously perched.

The only settlement on Coll is Arinagour, with three piers, shops, hotel, guest-house, school, post office, perfume factory and doctor. It is possible to charter boats locally for fishing trips and sightseeing. The island is ideal for walking and cycling, with lots of interesting nooks and crannies to explore. There are fine views eastwards to Mull,

*Breachacha Castle on the island of Coll, seat of the MacLeans of
Coll, now fully restored to its former glory.*

the Treshnish Islands and Staffa, and north to the Small Isles and Skye.

One of the most picturesque scenes in the Hebrides is at Sorisdale, at the north end of Coll, probably named for a Norseman who settled there soon after AD 1000. A single thatched cottage remains of what was once a thriving and populous settlement. Surrounding the sandy bay are boat 'noosts' for sheltering small boats during winter storms. Some of these may be of Norse date. In the sand dunes north of Sorisdale a 'beaker' burial, dating from the Bronze Age, was found after a series of storms in September 1976.

The north-east coast of the island, between Sorisdale and Arinagour, is an uninhabited wilderness, excellent for easy hill-walking or just wandering. The prehistoric fort at Dun Dulorichan, on an isolated steep-sided rocky outcrop overlooking the south-east end of Loch Airidh Raonuill is poorly preserved, but worth a visit for its setting.

The natural history of the island reflects a fairly wide range of habitats, and is typical of the Inner Hebrides. There is a small native population of greylag geese.

Coll has a rich archaeological heritage. Notable are the chambered cairn at Arinagour and the two standing stones at Totronald, mentioned by Johnson and Boswell who were stormbound here in 1773. The stones are known as Na Sgeulachan, 'the Tellers of Tales', and date probably from the Bronze Age – around 1500 BC. Both are granite slabs, aligned WNW–ESE, possibly indicating important positions in the movements of the sun and moon.

There several Iron Age forts; those at Dun an Achaidh and Feall Bay are best preserved. A feature of Dun an Achaidh is the marked contrast between the natural quartzite of the ridge on which it stands and the stones and boulders of Lewisian gneiss used in its construction. Casual finds from the site have included plain and decorated pottery, a slate whorl and a stone pounder. An alternative name for this fort is *Dun Bhorlum mhic Anlaimh righ Lochlinn* – 'the fort of the ridge of the son of Olaf, King of Norway'. Badly ruined, but in a spectacular location, is the fort of Dun Morbhaidh, on a small, craggy hill near the shore to the north-west of Cornaigbeg farm. Pottery with

A craggy Iron Age site at Dun Morbhibh, on the north-west coast of the island of Coll; animal-decorated pottery was found here.

A typical Hebridean 'dun' on the raised beach, on an isolated rocky site naturally defended on all sides, at An Casteal, Coll.

incised animal designs has been found here.

To the north of the road near the cattle grid at Kilbride farm are the remains of a hut-circle and enclosure. The hut-circle is fairly well-preserved, with the stone wall surviving to a height of two courses on the north side. The internal diameter of the hut was 14 feet (4.3m), while the wall, which probably supported a conical, thatched roof, is seven feet (2.2m) thick. The entrance faces east, and is just over three feet (1m) wide, with well-defined stone jambs.

Unusual in the islands, there is a souterrain at the Arnabost crossroads enquire locally to obtain access. It was discovered in 1855 and excavated in 1896 by the island's postmaster, Robert Sturgeon. There are several crannogs (fortified islands) in Coll's hill lochs.

The medieval parish church is at Killunaig, on the north-west coast, first recorded in 1433 when the parsonage and the vicarage belonged to the nunnery of Iona. There are fine views from the top of the sand dunes behind the church. In the dunes 885 feet (270m) west of the burial ground at Killunaig are two cists, dating from the Bronze Age, which when excavated in 1976 were found to contain the remains of three individuals.

The beaches on the west side of the island, especially at Killunaig, Hogh Bay and Feall Bay, are amongst the finest in the Hebrides. At Grishipoll, between Arnabost and Acha, there is a fine, though roofless, example of a mid-eighteenth century laird's house. It was built by Hugh MacLean, and occupied when he succeeded his brother as fourteenth laird of Coll in 1754. When James Boswell and Samuel Johnson stayed there in October 1773, it was tenanted by Sween McSween.

At the south end of the island is Breachacha Castle, in design comparable to Kissimul castle in Barra. In 1965 it was bought and restored by Major N. V. MacLean-Bristol, a descendant of the Macleans of Coll who owned it from 1631 to 1856, and is now used as the headquarters for an adventure-training school, the Project Trust, which sends 200 young people annually overseas in the year between school and university. Tours of the castle run in conjunction with some ferries. On certain days it is possible to spend three and a half hours on Coll on a day trip from

Tobermory or Oban. In the surrounding fields many rare breeds of sheep and cattle are kept. Nearby is a dilapidated eighteenth century mansion.

The population of the island was much greater in the past than it is now. In 1793 the First Statistical Account – a kind of inventory of all the parishes in Scotland – quotes a population of 1041. Already thirty-six people had emigrated to America, in 1792. Near Acha House is an abandoned Mill, with most of the original machinery intact. When it was built, in the nineteenth century, the population of the island justified such a major investment, reaching a peak of 1409 in 1841. Over the next twenty years, 700 people emigrated, mainly to Canada and Australia.

Agriculture is the main industry, with a little tourism. There are about 1000 beef cattle, 7000 sheep, and a few dairy cattle. One or two local fisherman make a precarious living from lobsters, clams and prawns. Tourism is still small-scale, mostly due to lack of accommodation coupled with an unattractive ferry timetable – it requires a high level of commitment to turn up at Oban pier at 6.00 am, especially if travelling from the south of England. But those who do come, come again and again and are not particularly keen to see the island changed. However, the declining and ageing local population desperately need to attract young couples with families, and the problem of providing them with employment is serious.

Tiree

Calmac ferries: Oban-Tiree (via Tobermory and Coll); passage time, 4 hours 15 minutes. On summer Fridays, direct Oban-Tiree service; passage time, 3 hours 15–30 minutes. Sailings three times/week in winter, four times/week in summer. Sailing days vary. Summer Sundays: Mallaig-Armadale-Tobermory-Coll-Tiree round trip.
Ferry information: For vehicle reservations contact Caledonian MacBrayne Ltd, The South Pier, Oban, Argyll. Tel: (0631) 62285, Fax: (0631) 66588. Most ferries leave Oban at 6.00 am. Overnight berths bookable on ferry. At present vehicles are unloaded by means of a side lift, but new roll-on, roll-of facilities are planned in the near future.
Local ferry office: The Pier, Scarinish, Isle of Tiree, Argyll. Tel: (087 92) 337.

Railhead: Oban.
Airport: Tiree Airport has daily flights to Glasgow Airport, operated by Loganair; flight time, 50 minutes.
Accommodation: Hotels, guest-houses, B & B, caravans, camping.
Tourist Information Centre: Oban, Mull & District Tourist Board, Bothwell House, Argyll Square, Oban, Argyll. Tel: (0631) 63122.

The island of Tiree lies in the Inner Hebrides, to the west of Mull. Reached by ferry from Oban, it is a popular destination for windsurfers. With a population of 800 on a land area of 29 square miles (74sq km), it is busier and much more fertile than its northern neighbour, Coll. The island is about 12 miles (19km) long and three miles (4.8km) wide. Tiree is a windswept, flat island, its level landscape broken only by sand dunes, occasional rocky knolls, and the hills of Ben Hynish (462ft/141m) and Beinn Hough (390ft/119m) at its western extremities. On the western skyline a massive dimpled military communications 'golfball' is prominent. In Gaelic Tiree was sometimes given the nickname *Tir fo Thuinn*, 'Land below the waves'. When seen from a distance the low ground disappears below the horizon, leaving the south-western hills stranded.

The long, flat sandy beaches all around the island mean that visiting windsurfers can always find somewhere to practise their sport. The locals were initially worried

Tiree's clean and unpolluted beaches have become famous in recent years as the venue for windsurfing championships.

Clach a'Choire, the 'ringing stone' near Balephetrish, Tiree, is a glacial eratic covered with Bronze Age cup-marks nearly four thousand years old.

The medieval church at Kirkapol, Tiree, with some fine carved stone grave-slabs in the burial ground.

about the influx of brightly coloured visitors with their strange obsession, but the years have mellowed suspicion on both sides and Tiree is now a regular venue for surfing championships.

The underlying bedrock is Lewisian gneiss, but windblown sand has allowed fertile, well-drained machair to cover most of the island. Tiree was known in Gaelic as the land of corn (*Tir-Iodh*) and supported a population of 4450 in 1831. Following famines and evictions the population declined to 2700 by 1881. At the height of the tourist season today it approaches the levels of the last century.

There are several interesting archaeological sites, including the excavated broch of Dun Mor Vaul; the finds are in the Hunterian Museum at Glasgow University. The broch sits on an outcrop of Lewisian gneiss on the north coast of Tiree, about 440 yards (400m) north of the township of Vaul. The rig and furrow marks of crofting agriculture are visible on the grassy areas around the rocky knoll on which the broch stands. Excavations showed the site to be complex, with an initial Iron Age occupation dating from around 500 BC. The broch itself, of which substantial walling remains, was probably built in the first century AD; it continued in use until AD 300. The wall was 10–13 feet (3–4m) thick and had a continuous gallery inside it, running almost the whole way round the building. The original height of the broch was 25–30 feet (7–9m), with perhaps three or four galleries on top of the surviving one at ground level. A stairway, of which only the first eleven steps survive, would have run up to the wall head by means of mural galleries. A ledge running round the inside wall and a ring of post-holes would have supported a wooden floor. In times of danger fifty to sixty people may have lived in the broch. It is one of the most impressive archaeological monuments anywhere in the Hebrides.

On the shore between Vaul and Balephetrish is a granite glacial erratic, the 'ringing stone', *Clach a'Choire* covered with over fifty Bronze Age cup marks. It makes a metallic sound when struck. There is a legend that if it ever shatters, or falls off the pedestal of small stones on which it rests, Tiree will sink beneath the waves.

*An Early Christian cross from the burial ground at Soroby, Tiree,
decorated front and back with intricately carved designs.*

Further west along this northern shore, above
Balephetrish farmhouse, is another poorly preserved
prehistoric fort, with a well inside the ruined walls.

The most spectacular island scenery is at the headland
of Kenavara, in Gaelic *Ceann a' Mhara*. On the headland
itself is a prehistoric fort, Dun nan Gall. All around are
massive sea cliffs, battered endlessly by Atlantic rollers. In
the breeding season, thousands of sea birds wheel
overhead, and seals play among the rocky shore. The
natural history of Tiree is typically Hebridean, with
abundant bird life and a profusion of wild flowers in the
spring, especially on the grassy coastal pastures known as
machair. One strange feature of the island is that there are
no rabbits.

Tiree has a long and interesting history. The Early
Christian Columban church was present on the island, and
has left traces at Kirkapol, in the form of simple Latin
crosses carved on rocks to mark the extent of the
consecrated ground. There are also two late medieval
chapels at Kirkapol, and some carved grave-slabs. After
the centuries of Norse rule, from AD 850 until 1150, Tiree
was part of the territory of Somerled, the founder of the
MacDonald Lords of the Isles. When the Lordship of the

Isles was abolished in 1493 and reverted to the Crown, Tiree was granted, in 1517, to the MacLeans of Duart (on Mull). The MacDonalds resisted and feuding continued for many years. The Campbells took over the island in 1674, after rising debts diminished the power of the MacLeans. Island House was built by the Earl of Argyll for his factor in 1748 at Loch an Eilein, Heylipol, on the site of an earlier stronghold.

In 1886 Scarinish was the scene of a confrontation between local crofters and the government. About 250 marines and fifty policemen were drafted on to the island to restore law and order. Eight crofters were arrested and sentenced to from four to six months imprisonment in Edinburgh. The relative prosperity of the island today is due in large measure to concessions won from the government, especially after the First World War.

The ferry terminal and main township is at Scarinish. The pier area at the west end of Gott Bay is rather unkempt, but the village half a mile (0.8km) away has interesting shops, offices, post office, bank and other services, and an old harbour. The islanders are proud of their secondary school, the smallest in the country. There are several crofting townships around the island, many with restored thatched houses. Balevullin has several brightly painted renovated traditional houses. The thick walls and rounded corners are perfectly adapted for the windy Hebridean environment.

At Hynish, at the southern tip of the island, there is an interesting harbour and signalling tower, containing relics and information about the lighthouse on Skerryvore, ten miles (16km) to the south-west. It was built in 1838–43 by Alan Stevenson, an uncle of the writer Robert Louis Stevenson. A large telescope is provided to facilitate viewing.

Tiree has a weather station, which regularly records more hours of sunshine here than at almost any other part of Britain. Its report comes right at the beginning of the 'coastal stations' listed on the BBC shipping forecast. Rainfall is well below the average for the west coast of Scotland, but there is no getting away from the fact that it is a windy place to live. The wind varies from strong to unrelenting, which is bad news for midges, the scourge of the Western Isles in the tourist season. Although Tiree's flatness is good news for cyclists, the wind more than compensates for the absence of hills.

The airport is in the middle of the island, in an area known as 'The Reef'. The strange name is a corruption of the Gaelic *ruighe*, 'summer pasture'. More than 4000 servicemen were stationed here during the Second World War. The airfield was built in 1941 on the site of a grass landing strip. Planes flew long patrols out over the Atlantic from Tiree. The island is littered with debris from the war years. Old huts, building foundations, gun emplacements and other bits and pieces are scattered around the island, though much has found a use around the island's many crofts.

The Small Isles:
Eigg, Muck, Rum, Canna

Calmac ferries: Mallaig-Eigg-Muck-Rum-Canna; passage time, Eigg 1 hour 30 minutes, Muck 2 hours 30 minutes, Rum 3–3 hours 30 minutes, Canna 4–4 hours 30 minutes. On summer Saturdays early morning ferry (5.00 am) sails Mallaig-Canna-Rum-Muck-Eigg.
Ferry information: No vehicles carried. Summer sailings, Mon., Wed., Fri., Sat; winter sailings, Mon., Wed. only. For timings contact Caledonian MacBrayne Ltd, The Ferry Terminal, Mallaig, PH41 4QB. On summer Saturdays there are two sailings from Mallaig, making it possible to spend either 9 hours 30 minutes on Canna, or 7 hours 30 minutes on Rum, 5 hours on Muck, or 3 hours 30 minutes on Eigg. At Eigg, Muck and Rum passengers are transferred to small boats as there are no suitable piers.

Railhead: Mallaig. Through connections to Fort William, Glasgow and London.
Airport: none.
Accommodation: very limited except on Rum. Contact Tourist Information Centre, Mallaig.
Tourist Information Centre: Mallaig. Tel: (0687) 2170. Fort William & Lochaber Tourist Board, Travel Centre, Fort William. Tel: (0397) 3781.

The Small Isles Parish consists of the islands of Eigg, Muck, Rum and Canna, which are located south-west of Skye and west of Mallaig, from where there is a passenger ferry. The islands, which are all inhabited, are all part of Highland Region. If small is beautiful, then this is the place to be. Although the populations of these communities are small, the islands are viable working units – just.

EIGG

The island of Eigg (Gaelic: *eige*, 'a hollow'), 6.5 by 4 miles (10.4 by 6.4km) in size, has been in the headlines quite a lot recently, due to the domestic difficulties of its laird. When placed on the market, it is expected to fetch over 1 million. The population is about thirty-five. In the 1950s there were

The Sgurr of Eigg is the island's most distinctive feature, easily identified for miles around.

thirty-five to forty children in the school. Now there are eight to ten. In the 1840s the population was over 500.

In 1577 practically the entire population of Eigg was suffocated in a cave by MacLeods from Skye. The atrocity took place in winter; the hideout was given away by footprints in the snow. The MacLeods piled brushwood at the entrance to the cave and set fire to it. The smoke killed all within – about 395 men, women and children, all tenants of the MacDonald laird. MacDonald's Cave is half a mile (0.8km) south-west of the pier. In Early Christian times a monastery was established on the island by St Donnan, who was killed there by islanders.

Looming over the harbour and the main settlement of Galmisdale (shop and post office) is the 'sgurr' of Eigg, An Sgurr, a distinctively shaped ridge of columnar pitchstone identifiable from far and wide, reaching a height of 1290 feet (393m). There is a superb view from the summit. It is home to a colony of Manx shearwater, which burrow into the ground for nesting. At the foot of An Sgurr are the abandoned townships of Upper and Lower Grulin. Over 100 men, women and children from Grulin were evicted to make room for sheep in the 1850s, and moved to Nova

The Scottish mainland as seen from the island of Eigg.

Scotia, in Canada. At the north end of the island is the small crofting township of Cleasdale, on the Bay of Laig. In 1841, when the population of the island was 546, there were over 150 people there. Now there are fewer than twenty. At Camas Sgiotaig there are strange sandstone rock formations, and singing sands.

MUCK

Muck is the tiniest of the Small Isles, less than two miles (3.2km) by a mile (1.6km), with a land area of 1586 acres (642 hectares). The high point is Beinn Airein, 451 feet (138m). Muck is 2.5 miles (4km) south-west of its neighbour, Eigg. Its name comes from the Gaelic *Eilean a muic*, 'the island of the pig'. During the Napoleonic wars 280 people lived on Muck, working in the kelp industry, but by 1826 the industry collapsed, and with it the economies of Muck and many other islands. In 1861 the population was fifty-eight; today it is twenty-six. There is a traditional laird's house at Gallanach, and a guesthouse at Port Mor.

The Small Isles ferry, Lochmor, *which sails from Mallaig to serve the islands of Rum, Eigg, Muck and Canna.*

On the east coast of Arran is the quiet harbour of Lamlash, with the Holy Isle in the background.

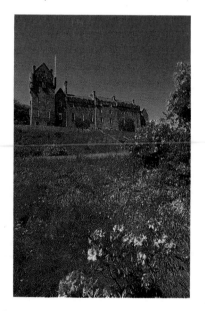

Brodick Castle, Arran, once the home of the Dukes of Hamilton, now gifted to the National Trust for Scotland, along with its gardens.

The peaceful little harbour at Port Bannatyne, on the north side of Rothesay Bay, at the entrance to the Kyles of Bute.

Caledonian MacBrayne's new Gigha ferry at Ardminish; an extended summer service has opened the island up to day-trippers from Kintyre.

Looking towards the island of Rum from above the village on Canna, in the Parish of the Small Isles.

An Coroghan, Canna; spectacular coastal scenery on an is' owned by the National Trust for Scotland

One of the many carefully preserved and restored 'black' houses on the flat, windy island of Tiree.

The last thatched house on Coll, at Sorisdale, once a thriving village at the north tip of the island.

Looking over the sheltered waters of Loch na Keal to Ben More, the highest mountain on Mull.

Looking across to Lismore and the hills of Morvern from the mainland at Port Appin, from where a small passenger ferry crosses frequently.

The Sanctuary Cross in the middle of the tidal strand between Colonsay and Oronsay, marking the boundary of the lands of Oronsay Priory.

Aerial view of Tobermory, the chief town on the island of Mull, with ferry connections to Oban, Coll, Tiree and Ardnamurchan.

The medieval castle at Dunivaig, on the sheltered south-east coast of Islay, the main fortress and naval base of the Lords of the Isles.

over the settlement and ferry terminal at Scalasaig, Isle of Colonsay, across to the islands of Jura and Islay.

RUM

Calmac and the Ordnance Survey still spell this island's name 'Rhum' – though the 'h' was reputedly introduced in Victorian times to take account of sensibilities over strong liquor. It also makes the name look less 'English' and more 'foreign'. Properly pronounced 'Room', the name may derive from the Norse *Röm oe*, 'wide island'. Measuring six by six and a half miles (9.6 by 10.4km), it is the largest of the Small Isles.

Today Rum looks like a trackless wilderness, but it once supported over 300 people. Most of them ended up in Canada, replaced by 8000 sheep. In 1888 it was bought by John Bullough of Oswaldtwistle, who made a fortune in the textile industry, designing machinery. His son Sir George Bullough took over in 1891, and built Kinloch Castle, a massive late-Victorian mansion on which no expense was spared. The red sandstone was brought from the island of Arran, in the Clyde. The fittings are opulent. In 1957 his widow Lady Monica sold the island to the Nature Conservancy Council (NCC), who now run it as an enormous outdoor laboratory and research station, supporting a population of about forty.

On the west side of Rum is what has all the appearance of a Greek temple but is in fact the Bullough family mausoleum. To say it looks out of place is an understatement. The NCC has maintained Kinloch Castle as an Edwardian mansion, and runs it in the summer as an up-market hotel. Cheap hostel accommodation is also available. Although Rum is an artificial community wholly dependent on the scientific staff and their families, it is an interesting and congenial place to spend a week, if you are interested in natural history and outdoor pursuits.

Ongoing studies of the red deer population of Rum are providing crucial information for the future of a venison industry in the Highlands. The thousands of breeding sea birds are constantly studied, and over 130,000 pairs of Manx shearwater nest on the mountain tops. The mountains have Norse names Orval, Askival (2664ft/813m), Hallival, Ruinsival, Barkeval, Trallval. The last of these takes its name from the troll of Norse mythology, which

Ponies at Kinloch Castle, Rum, which was built at vast expense by Sir George Bullough, now preserved as a monument to Edwardian opulence.

visiting Norsemen heard at night in these hills. What they really heard was the eerie call of the Manx shearwater. In recent years the white-tailed sea eagle has been re-introduced to the Hebrides, from Norway, and is slowly spreading outwards from Rum.

In recent years archaeologists have found evidence of human occupation on Rum before 6000 BC, in the form of thousands of flint and bloodstone flakes, at a site near Kinloch. 60 million years ago, Rum was a volcano.

CANNA

With a population of about twenty on an island five miles (8km) long by one mile (1.6km) wide, Canna is the most westerly of the Small Isles. The deep water harbour and pier are sheltered by the tidal island of Sanday. There are spectacular views to Rum and Skye. The high point of the island is Carn a Ghaill, 690 feet (210m). Above the pier is Compass Hill (458ft/140m); the highly metallic rock affects navigation in its vicinity.

Like Rum, Canna is an artificial community, owned by the National Trust for Scotland. The folklorist and

Gallanach Farm on Muck, with the island of Eigg visible in the distance.

Gaelic scholar John Lorne Campbell bought the island in 1938, but has recently handed it over to the National Trust for Scotland, from whom limited accommodation is available. Dr Campbell has assembled one of the finest collections of books on the Hebrides, Highland history and Gaelic culture generally. Under his regime the island was run as a single working farm, and it is hoped that this will continue, despite some controversy about how the new owners are discharging their responsibilities.

On a fine summer Saturday, it is possible to join the day trippers from Mallaig and spend over nine hours ashore on Canna, which is just long enough to have a good wander, a picnic, and enjoy the panoramic views before catching the ferry back to Mallaig. A long day though, with a five o'clock start from Mallaig, arriving back at 7.30 pm.

THE HEBRIDES

Butt of Lewis

ATLANTIC
OCEAN

Barvas

Shawbost
Carloway
Stornoway

Lewis

North

Minch

To Ulla

H
e
b
r
i
d
e
s

Tarbert
Kyles Scalpay

Harris
Scalpay

Shiant Is.

Pabbay
Berneray

S
o
u
n
d

o
f

H
a
r
r
i
s

L
i
t
t
l
e

M
i
n
c
h

Staffin

L. Torridon

North
Uist
Lochmaddy

Uig

O
u
t
e
r

Dunvegan
Portree

Skye

Raasay

Benbecula

Sconser

Ky
Loc

South
Uist

Cuillin
Hills

Broadford

Kylea

Lochboisdale

Soay
Elgol

Eriskay

Barra

Canna

Cuillin

Sound

Armadale

Castlebay
Vatersay

Rum

Mallai

Sandray

Eigg

Mingulay
Barra Head

Muck

Ardnamurchan Pt.

0   20 miles
0   30 kms

Coll

To Oban

Skye

Calmac ferries: Kyle of Lochalsh-Kyleakin; frequent sailings, passage time, 5 minutes, no reservations necessary; 24-hour service from Easter 1991. Uig-Tarbert/Lochmaddy; passage time 1 hour 45 minutes–2 hours 15 minutes. Mallaig-Armadale; passage time, 30 minutes. Summer Sundays Mallaig-Armadale-Tobermory-Coll-Tiree round trip.
A private seasonal vehicle ferry service operates from Glenelg to Kylerhea.
Ferry information: For vehicle reservations contact Caldonian MacBrayne Ltd, The Ferry Terminal, Uig, Isle of Skye. Tel: (047 042) 219, Fax: (047 042) 387.
Local ferry offices: Armidale, Tel: (047 14) 248; Kyleakin, Tel: (0599) 4482.

Railheads: Kyle of Lochalsh and Mallaig.
Airport: private airstrip at Broadford
Car and bicycle hire: enquire at TIC, Portree.
Island newspaper: *West Highland Free Press.*
Accommodation: Hotels, guest-houses, B & B, self-catering, caravans and camping.
Tourist Information Centre: Meall House, Portree, Isle of Skye. Tel: (0478) 2137. Also Broadford and Kyle of Lochalsh.

The island of Skye (Gaelic: *An t-Eilean Sgitheanach*) is a large island covering 535 square miles (1370sq km), with a complicated topography featuring fingers of land separated by sea lochs penetrating far inland, forming 350 miles (560km) of coastline. Loch Snizort, Loch Dunvegan, Loch Harport, Loch Eishort, Loch Ainort, Loch Sligachan – the names reveal the mixture of Norse and Gaelic culture which has influenced the island over many centuries.

It is possible to run up a hefty mileage during a week's holiday on Skye. It is the largest of the Inner Hebrides, measuring 50 miles (80km) long and from seven to 25 miles (11–40km) broad.

Geologically, Skye is renowned for its lava landscapes, especially in the Trotternish area, where the Old Man of Storr and the unusual formations of the Quirang attract many visitors. Also greatly admired, whenever visible through the ubiquitous mist, are the Cuillins, jagged mountains of hard gabbro beloved by generations of

Sligachan Bridge and the Cuillins, a rendezvous for generations of climbers in the misty Isle of Skye.

The unearthly landscape of the Quirang, in the Trotternish district of the Isle of Skye, is caused by volcanic landforms.

climbers. The Red Cuillins, made of only slightly less hard granite, have eroded into more rounded shapes, and have slopes of scree. The fertility of some parts of the island derives from underlying sandstones and limestones which surface around the volcanic rocks.

A rich variety of archaeological and historical monuments testifies to Skye's long and turbulent history. Of particular interest are the brochs of Dun Ardtreck near Carbost and Dun Beag, just west of Bracadale, both very neatly built using square-sided facing-stones. These were originally stone towers up to 30 feet (9m) high. Clach Ard, Tote, is a Pictish symbol stone, unusual in the Hebrides.

Skye is part of the heartland of Gaelic culture, with a large proportion of the population of 8500 speaking the Gaelic language in everyday life. As in other parts of the Hebrides, this culture is under threat, particularly from incomers, but there is a resurrection of interest in Gaelic culture, assisted by a Gaelic college (Sabhal Mor Ostaig), Gaelic poetry (e.g. Sorley MacLean), Gaelic rock music (e.g. Run Rig), a local newspaper (*The West Highland Free Press*), together with economic support from the Highlands and Islands Enterprise (previously HIDB) and spiritual underpinning from the extreme Sabbatarian Free Church.

Local museums at Luib, Colbost, Glendale and Kilmuir help interpret crofting society to visitors.

Kilmuir burial ground has the grave of Flora MacDonald, and a monument to the most famous lady in Skye's long history. The monument has Dr Johnson's epitaph engraved on it 'Her name will be mentioned in history and if courage and fidelity be virtues, mentioned with honour'. It was she who helped Bonnie Prince Charlie escape capture after the defeat at Culloden in 1746, by transporting him in a boat from North Uist, 'over the sea to Skye'. After Flora's part in the escape became known, she was arrested and spent almost a year in the Tower of London. After a busy life, including some dozen years in North Carolina, she returned to her husband's house at Kingsburgh, and died in Skye in 1790. It is said that her funeral was the largest ever witnessed in the Highlands.

Also in the Kilmuir graveyard are some members of the MacArthur family who were hereditary pipers to the MacDonalds at Duntulm Castle. Kilmuir also has a major visitor attraction in the restored thatched cottages making up the Skye Museum of Island Life, opened in 1965. Here the way of life of a traditional crofting community of the past can be experienced.

Another famous piping family was the MacCrimmons of Borreraig, hereditary pipers to the MacLeods of Dunvegan for over 200 years. They operated a College of Piping, with a course of instruction lasting three years. A cairn commemorates their activities, and every year in August a special piping competition is held in their honour in the drawing room of Dunvegan Castle. Classical piping music, traditionally played only by the greatest pipers, is known as pibroch or *piobaireachd*, or *Ceol mor*, 'the great music', pronounced 'kyoll more'. A new Piping Centre at the old school in Borreraig tells the story of the bagpipes, which have survived their banning after Culloden to be the internationally recognised symbol of the Highland Scot.

In the nineteenth century the native culture came under serious threat, with an estimated emigration of 30,000 between 1840 and 1888. In 1882 the Battle of the Braes saw a confrontation over grazing rights between local farmers in the Braes district near Portree and fifty Glasgow

Glendale, a sadly depopulated district of Skye, looking out over
Loch Pooltiel to the mountains of North Uist.

policemen imported to keep control. After a pitched battle
gunboats were sent and a force of marines landed at Uig.
After a public outcry a Royal Commission was established
by Gladstone, which resulted in the Crofters Act of 1886,
providing security of tenure at a fair and controlled rent.
This system, which replaced the original communal
townships, remains in force today.

The principal residence of the MacDonalds of Sleat
from 1815 was Armadale Castle, the surviving portion of
which has been renovated and opened to the public as the
Clan Donald Centre. Previous MacDonald castles included
Dun Scaich, on the west side of the Sleat peninsula, Knock
Castle or Castle Camus, also in Sleat, and Duntulm, a
spectacular site at the north end of Trotternish, abandoned
about 1730. Dunvegan Castle, the ancient seat of the
MacLeods of Dunvegan and Harris, occupies a rocky site
on the east shore of Loch Dunvegan. The keep dates to the
fourteenth century. In part of the later eighteenth century
buildings is an exhibition covering the history of the Clan
MacLeod, including the famous 'Fairy Flag', a silk banner
of eastern origin thought to convey protection on the clan.

Uig Bay, Isle of Skye, from where the Calmac ferry sails to Tarbert, Harris and Lochmaddy, North Uist.

Skye has five ferry terminals connecting it to the mainland and the surrounding islands. The main crossing is from the railhead at Kyle of Lochalsh to Kyleakin, a short, five-minute crossing eventually to be replaced by a toll bridge. From 1991 Calmac will be operating a twenty-four-hour service on this route. This is where the Norwegian king Haakon anchored his longships in 1263, on his way to the fiasco of the Battle of Largs; the place-name commemorates his visit. A few miles to the south is a seasonal ferry connection from Glenelg to Kylerhea – another short crossing through treacherous, tidal races. At the southern end of the Sleat (pronounced 'slate') peninsula there is a ferry connecting Armadale to Mallaig, another railhead, with connections through Fort William to Glasgow and London. This ferry only takes vehicles in the summer, but operates as a passenger service the rest of the year. At the opposite end of Skye, from the harbour of Uig in the Trotternish peninsula, there are ferry connections to the Outer Hebrides (Tarbert on Harris, and Lochmaddy on North Uist). Another short crossing connects Sconser on Skye to the island of Raasay.

'Over the sea to Skye'? The Calmac ferry at Kyleakin, now linked to
Kyle of Lochalsh on the mainland by a short, 24-hour ferry service,
will one day be replaced by a road bridge.

All these ferries, and the island's extensive road system, are stretched beyond capacity in the summer tourist season, when over one million visitors sail 'over the sea to Skye'. Although crofting and fishing still form the basis of the island's economy, tourism and light industry, including electronics, are now vitally important. There is a famous whisky distillery at Carbost, the Talisker Malt Whisky Distillery, established in 1833. Most of its production is blended for export. There are guided tours during the tourist season.

Portree, with a population of over 1000, is the main town, with hotels, shops, banks, and all the usual services, including a Tourist Information Centre. Its name derives from a visit by King James V in 1540, on an expedition to quell insurrections among the rebellious population of the Western Isles. In this aim he was not notably successful.

Skye Week, an annual festival of culture and leisure events, is one of the major events of the year. From Broadford (900), a lively village with craft shops and an annual folk festival, a scenic road leads eventually to Elgol, from where there is a fine view of the Cuillin ridge. A track leads from Elgol to the Sligachan Hotel past Loch Coruisk. There are many other thriving crofting townships throughout the island.

There are many scenic and interesting areas in Skye of outstanding natural beauty, but none is more spectacular than the Neist peninsula west of Dunvegan. On the western tip of Skye is the Neist Point lighthouse, overlooking towering cliffs of sea birds. Nearby are the 967 foot (295m) cliffs of Waterstein Head. Far out to the west are North and South Uist, and Benbecula. In the Sleat peninsula, the small village of Isleornsay is very picturesque and attractive, situated in a more fertile, sheltered, landscape. The nearby small tidal island of Ornsay has a ruined chapel and an unmanned lighthouse.

Raasay

Calmac ferries: Sconser (Skye)-Raasay; passage time, 15 minutes.
Ferry information: For vehicle reservations contact Ferrymaster, Raasay, Tel: (0478) 62226. No Sunday service.

Railhead: Kyle of Lochalsh; ferry to Kyleakin (Skye), then by road to Sconser.
Airport: none. Nearest airstrip is at Broadford (Skye).
Accommodation: Hotel, limited B & B, self-catering, camping.
Tourist Information Centre: Portree, Isle of Skye. Tel: (0478) 2137.

The island of Raasay lies east of Skye, separated from the Trotternish Peninsula by the Sound of Raasay. The mainland district of Applecross is eight miles (12.8km) to the east. Raasay is 13 miles (21km) long and up to three miles (5km) wide, with a population of 180 in 30 square miles (77sq km). It is a hilly island, rising in the centre to the flat-topped Dun Caan (1456ft/444m), where Boswell 'danced a Highland dance' in 1773.

There is a short ferry connection to Sconser on the Isle of Skye. The principle settlement is Inverarish, between the ferry slip and Raasay House, where the Macleod laird, his wife and large family (three sons and ten daughters) entertained Boswell and Dr Johnson in lavish style. They expressed in rather flowery prose what generations of visitors to the Hebrides have felt 'Such a seat of hospitality amid the winds and waters fill the imagination with a delightful contrariety of images'! Raasay House stands on the site of a tower house built in 1549. On the east side of the island is Brochel Castle, built by MacLeods of Lewis in the fifteenth century.

The original Raasay House was burned by government troops after Culloden. Because the outlawed Bonnie Prince Charlie was given refuge on Raasay, 300 houses were burned, 280 cows and 700 sheep slaughtered, several horses shot, and most of the island's boats were holed and sunk.

After John MacLeod of Raasay sold the island in 1843, it passed through the hands of numerous owners, none of whom were able to reverse a trend of emigration, depopulation and poverty which continued until recent

Looking back from the island of Raasay to the mountains of the neighbouring island of Skye.

Raasay ferry, provided by Caledonian MacBrayne since 1976, is the island's lifeline; it sails from Sconser, on the Isle of Skye.

Terraced houses at Inverarish, Raasay, built for ironstone mineworkers at the nearby mineworkings, long abandoned.

times. Raasay House was run as a hotel from 1937 to 1960, then was allowed to collapse into a dilapidated ruin. It is now used as the base for an outdoor adventure school. There is a hotel and youth hostel. Raasay is strictly Sabbatarian, due to the influence of the Free Church. The poet Sorley Maclean is a native of Raasay. His brother Calum, who died in 1960 at the age of forty-five, was the author of *The Highlands*, one of the most evocative and perceptive accounts of the Highlands ever written.

The two miles (3.2km) of road joining Brochel to Arnish are the work of one man, Calum MacLeod, who died in 1988 soon after building 'Calum's Road' single-handed over a period variously estimated at ten to fifteen years. With just a pick and shovel and a wheelbarrow, and a manual on road-making which cost him £ 0.25, he decided to build the road himself after the local council turned down his requests for a proper access to his home. Raasay Community Council decided to honour his achievement with a cairn, which was unveiled in 1990, with a suitable plaque in Gaelic and English.

*Looking across to the Isle of Skye from Raasay; historically the two
islands were always closely connected.*

Caledonian MacBrayne's Suilven *loading at Stornoway for the two-hour crossing across The Minch to Ullapool.*

Carloway broch was built two thousand years ago, a bell-shaped tower of dry-stone construction, on the west coast of Lewis.

Lewis

Calmac ferries: Ullapool-Stornoway; passage time, 3 hours 30 minutes.
Ferry information: For vehicle reservations contact Caledonian MacBrayne, The Ferry Terminal, Ullapool, Ross-shire. Tel: (0854) 2358.
Or, Uig-Tarbert (Harris); passage time 1.75 hours, then by road to Stornoway.
Local ferry office: The Ferry Terminal, Stornoway, Isle of Lewis. Tel (0851) 2361, Fax: (0851) 5523.

Railhead: Inverness; connecting bus to Ullapool.
Airport: Stornoway Airport has daily flights to Glasgow, operated by British Airways; flight time, 70 minutes. Loganair has connecting flights to Benbecula and Barra.
Island newspaper: *Stornoway Gazette.*
Accommodation: Hotels, guest-houses, B & B, self-catering, caravans and camping.
Tourist Information Centre: No 4 South Beach Street, Stornoway, Isle of Lewis. Tel: (0851) 3088.

The 'island' of Lewis (Gaelic: *Leodhas*, 'marshy') makes up the northern two-thirds of the most northerly island in the Outer Hebrides; Harris lies to the south, divided from its larger and more populous northern neighbour by Loch Seaforth and Loch Resort. Lewis has a land area of 680 square miles (1741sq km), and a population of 21,400.

Stornoway is the largest town in the Hebrides, and the administrative capital of the Western Isles, which today are ruled by Comhairle nan Eilean, the Islands' Council. With a population of nearly 6000, it has a fine, natural deep-water harbour. A ferry service connects with Ullapool, on the Scottish mainland, and Stornoway Airport is linked by scheduled services with Benbecula, Barra and Glasgow. Stornoway has some interesting buildings, notably Lews Castle, built with money made from opium and tea by Sir James Matheson, founder with another Scot of the firm of Jardine Matheson & Co.

Geologically, Lewis is the most interesting of the Outer Hebrides. The underlying rock is Lewisian gneiss, the oldest rock in Europe, at 2900 million years over half

A distant view of Stornoway, capital of the Hebrides, ferry terminal for Lewis, fishing port, and sabbatarian centre of the Free Church.

the age of the earth itself. Around Barvas, on the west side of Lewis, is a large exposure of granite, while around Stornoway is Torridonian sandstone. There is evidence in glacial striations on rocky outcrops of at least two ice ages, while the most recent geological deposition is the blanket peat which covers much of today's landscape but started to form only 5000 years ago.

Lewis is well known for its spectacular archaeological monuments, notably the bronze age standing stones at Callanish. The concentration of Bronze Age archaeological remains around the shores of Loch Roag, on the west coast of Lewis, suggests a regional centre of considerable significance in the second millenium BC. More than twenty sites have been recorded in this area, mainly stone circles and standing stones, but beyond doubt the finest monument and the centre of this ritual landscape is the site at Callanish itself. The forty-seven surviving stones, which date from around 1800 BC, are arranged in a cruciform pattern, measuring 405 feet (124m) from north to south and 140 feet (43m) from east to west. The tallest stone is

Fishing boats in Stornoway harbour; still an important fishing port despite recent troubles in the fishing industry.

over 15 feet (4.5m) in height. The true height of the stones was not appreciated until 1857, when five feet (1.5m) of peat which had accumulated since the end of the Bronze Age was removed.

Most of the stones are slabs of Lewisian gneiss. The natural grain of this rock gives the stones an ancient and eerie appearance, especially at dusk. The lower parts of the stones, which were buried in the peat, are paler. Controversial theories about the archaeo-astronomical use of standing stones appear to have slowly gained acceptance in recent years. There are many other stone circles and single standing stones from the same period. At Ballantrushal, on the west coast of Lewis just north of Barvas, the tallest standing stone in the Hebrides (19ft/5.8m high) overlooks the sea.

The dry-stone broch tower of Dun Carloway, on the west coast of the Isle of Lewis, is one of the best preserved examples of this type of late first millenium BC Iron Age homestead. In places the walls survive almost to their original height of 30 feet (9m), but the main feature of

interest is that the collapse of the northern side of the broch
has revealed, in section, the way in which the tower was
built. Details of the entrance with its guard cell, the hollow-
wall construction with internal staircases, and scarcement
ledge supporting a floor, are all clearly visible.

West of Callanish is the township of Uig, where a
magnificent Norse chess set of walrus ivory, dating from
the twelfth century, was found in the sand dunes in 1831.
Much reproduced, the original pieces were divided between
the British Museum in London and the Royal Scottish
Museum in Queen Street, Edinburgh. The King, Queen,
Bishop, Knight and Castle depict a medieval monarch and
his entourage, defended by Viking warrior pawns. These
are particularly fearsome, depicted biting hard on the edge
of their shields, eyes popping, in true Viking 'berserk'
fashion.

The extent of Viking domination in Lewis is revealed
by a study of place-names, many of which, including Uig
(Norse: *vik*, 'a bay') are of Norse origin. Many fine
artefacts of the period have been found on Viking-age
archaeological sites, including distinctive 'tortoise'-shaped
brooches, bone pins, and portable scales for itinerant
traders in precious metals. But the Uig chess set is the most
superb of all the finds from Viking Scotland. It represents
the final flourishing of Norse settlement in the Western
Isles, for shortly afterwards Somerled the son of Gillebride
defeated a Norse naval force and re-established Celtic
control of Norse territories. The Western Isles were first
raided by Vikings in the ninth century and then settled
extensively by Norse colonists. Legally, the Western Isles
were under Norwegian sovereignty until 1266.

Not far from Stornoway, the medieval chapel on the
Eye peninsula, dedicated to St Columba, is an important
ecclesiastical site. At the Butt of Lewis, the northern tip of
the island, is an important lighthouse. Outside the nearby
township of Eoropie is the restored twelfth century church
of St Moluag (*Teampull Mholuidh*).

To the west of Barvas is the township of Arnol, where
there is a small folk museum in a black house (*tigh dubh*),
last occupied in 1964. The walls are six feet thick, and the
roof was thatch over turf. There was no chimney, but

smoke from a peat fire in the middle of the floor escaped through the roof. This architecture, apparently primitive, was in fact better adapted to Hebridean wind and rain than the modern bungalows now seen throughout the islands.

On the road to Point, to the east of Stornoway, stands a monument to the saddest disaster ever to befall the Hebrides, where the ebb and flow of history has witnessed many tragic scenes. In 1919 the Admiralty yacht *Iolaire*, carrying 260 naval ratings returning to their villages from service in the Great War, foundered near Arnish Point early on New Year's Day, with the loss of 208 lives. Every village in the island, indeed, almost every home, was affected. Combined with the death toll of the war, and the emigrations which followed it, the *Iolaire* disaster affected succeeding generations profoundly. Its influence can still be traced.

The economy of Lewis is still based on the traditional industries of crofting, fishing, and tweed, despite various attempts to broaden the industrial base. The Highland and Islands Development Board (now HIE) has done much to encourage the island's economy, despite some spectacular failures. The growth of co-operatives and craft associations are evidence of the realisation that in a fragile community co-operation is essential. Unemployment figures are well above the national average, and the emigration of young people to the mainland and beyond is a perennial problem. Unfortunately, Stornoway is showing signs of following mainland trends as regards social problems.

Although the Harris Tweed industry has had its ups and downs in recent years, there is now an increasing demand from the fashion industry for quality tweed. To qualify as Harris Tweed, cloth must bear the orb trademark of the Harris Tweed Association, founded in 1909, and be made in the Outer Hebrides from virgin Scottish wool, woven on handlooms in the weavers' own homes.

Tweed is hard-wearing, warm, water-resistant – and fashionable. The cloth is produced in rolls of 38 weaver's yards (each of 72inches/1.83m), 28.5 inches (0.72m) wide. About 650 home weavers produce 4.5 million yards (4.1 million metres) of cloth annually. Traditional Gaelic 'waulking' songs arose out of the communal treatment of

Drying peats for winter fuel on the Isle of Lewis, where peat-cutting is still an important community activity.

the finished cloth.

Attempts to rationalise the industry by concentrating production in a factory in Stornoway met with almost total opposition from the weavers. But since 1934 the wool has been dyed, carded and spun in Stornoway. The hand looms are often housed in sheds or outhouses on crofts, leaving the operators free to look after their sheep, cut peat, and tend the croft.

Although Lewis is now the centre of the tweed industry, where weaving is often carried on by men, it had its origins in Harris, where the Earl of Dunmore at Amhuinnsuidhe Castle asked one of the local traditional weavers to copy some Murray tartan for his army's kilts. The pioneers were Marion and Christina Macleod of Strond, originally from the island of Pabbay, known as the 'Paisley' sisters because they were sent there for training by the Dowager Countess of Dunmore, Catherine Herbert, a daughter of the Earl of Pembroke.

The history of the Harris Tweed industry is displayed at An Clachan, Leverburgh. It is also described in detail in Francis Thompson's *Harris Tweed: the story of a Hebridean industry*.

Lewis is the most powerful bastion of Gaelic life and

culture surviving, in which the promotion of the Gaelic
language through Gaelic broadcasting and publishing is all
important. Radio nan Eilean, the Gaelic local radio station
run by the BBC, Gaelic television programmes, constantly
expanding, and the Stornoway publisher Acair are all
important influences in island culture. One of the finest
evocations of island life is *Devil in the wind*, by Charles
Macleod. The foremost Celtic scholar of the present
generation is a Lewisman, Professor Derick Thomson,
while the Gaelic (and English) poet and novelist Iain
Crichton Smith has a deservedly international reputation.
Comhairle nan Eilean's bilingual policy is very supportive
of Gaelic culture.

The sabbatarianism of the Free Church has proved
controversial in recent years, especially as regards Sunday
ferry sailings and public use of council-owned facilities. In
Lewis, the Free Church is still immensely powerful, the
issue being inextricably linked with the very survival of
Gaelic culture in all its richness.

Tarbert, Harris, the Caledonian MacBrayne ferry terminal linking Lewis and Harris with Lochmaddy, North Uist and Uig in the Isle of Skye.

Luskentyre, on the west coast of South Harris, an area of long, sandy beaches and inland wilderness.

Harris

Calmac ferries: Uig (Skye)-Tarbert; passage time, 1 hour 45 minutes.
Lochmaddy (North Uist)-Tarbert; passage time, 1 hour 45 minutes.
Ferry information: For vehicle reservations contact Caledonian
MacBrayne, The Ferry Terminal, Uig, Isle of Skye. Tel: (047 042)
219, Fax: (047 042) 387.
Local ferry office: The Ferry Terminal, Tarbert, Isle of Harris. Tel:
(0859) 2444, Fax: (0859) 2017.

Railhead: Kyle of Lochalsh; ferry to Kyleakin, then by road to Uig
(Skye).
Airport: Stornoway Airport has daily flights to Glasgow, operated by
British Airways. Loganair has connecting flights to Benbecula and
Barra.
Island newspaper: *Stornoway Gazette.*
Accommodation: Hotels, guest-houses, B & B, self-catering.
Tourist Information Centre: The Pier, Tarbert, Isle of Harris. Tel:
(0859) 2011.

The 'island' of Harris (Gaelic: *Na Hearadh*), is not an
island at all: together with Lewis it forms the largest
and most northerly of the Western Isles, Harris taking up
the southern third. The long sea lochs of Loch Seaforth
and Loch Resort divide the two districts. With a land area
of 90 square miles (230sq km) and a population of 2400,
Harris has a landscape which in places is almost
mountainous – very different from the flat, peaty lands of
Lewis. Clisham (2622ft/800m) is the highest hill in the
Outer Hebrides. Around it is some of the finest unspoilt
wilderness to be found anywhere in Scotland. Archaeological monuments and Norse place-names dot the
landscape.

The largest town and ferry terminal is at Tarbert,
which is connected by Caledonian MacBrayne's ferries to
Lochmaddy on North Uist and Uig on the Isle of Skye. A
passenger ferry plies from Leverburgh on Harris to
Newtonferry on North Uist. Another ferry serves the
offshore island of Scalpay.

One of Scotland's architectural gems is St Clement's
church, at Rodel, on the south-east corner of Harris.
Although it has been restored on several occasions, most

recently in 1873, most of the walls and the greater part of the tower are medieval, dating from the early sixteenth century. The windows are square-headed, except for the east window, which has a pointed arch with three trefoil-headed panels, above which is a wheel window with six spokes.

St Clement's is the finest pre-Reformation church in the Western Isles, and is memorable also for two magnificent medieval tombs built into its south wall. Rodel was the burial place for many of the MacLeods of Dunvegan and Harris, and the tomb of Alexander MacLeod of Dunvegan (also known as Alasdair Crotach) is an outstanding example of medieval stone carving. It was built in 1528, although curiously, Alexander did not die for another twenty years. His tomb consists of a stone effigy in chain mail and plate armour, lying with his head on a stone pillow. Behind the stone figure is a recessed arch decorated with panels illustrating a variety of scenes, including ecclesiasatical and biblical figures, a castle, a galley under sail, and a hunting scene, with men holding hunting dogs observing a group of deer. Because this tomb was built into the fabric of the church in the Middle Ages, and has never been subject to the ravages of Hebridean weather, the carvings have a freshness and detail rarely seen.

There are many other interesting architectural details in St Clement's church, including a carving of St Clement himself, with a bull's head beneath his feet, and a *sheila-na-gig* – a nude female figure, with a child, in a crouched attitude, blatantly displaying her vagina. It is thought that the purpose of such figures was to attract the attention of the satanic spirits, representing the evils and temptations of life, who would follow worshippers into the building.

The recent history of Harris is closely bound up with that of Lewis; both now form part of the all-purpose local authority administered from Stornoway by Comhairle nan Eilean, the Islands' Council. Much of present day attitudes towards local government and administration are conditioned by the era of Lord Leverhulme, the soap magnate, who bought Lewis and Harris in 1918–19 and proceeded to introduce ideas of social engineering which unfortunately met with a mixed reception and came to an abrupt end with

Rodel Church, Harris, the undisputed architectural gem of the Hebrides, houses a fine collection of medieval carved grave-stones.

his death in 1925. His 'Lewis & Harris Welfare & Development Company Limited' was an early version of the local Enterprise Trusts which are now in fashion again.

William Hesketh Lever, 1st Viscount Leverhulme, was born in 1851, the son of a Bolton soapmaker. He founded Port Sunlight in 1888 and Lever Brothers in 1890. His international business empire, Unilever, brought him fame and fortune. In 1918 he bought Lewis and Harris, and in the next five years spent 875,000, intending to redeem the islands from poverty and create wealth for the islanders through enterprise and the exploitation of the natural resources of the sea.

He bough fishing boats, and built a cannery, ice-factory, roads and bridges, and a light railway. He planned to use spotter planes to locate herring shoals, and created MacFisheries, his own chain of retail fish shops. A full account of his activities can be found in Nigel Nicolson's *Lord of the Isles.*

In 1923 he was forced to abandon his plans for Lewis, and gifted 64,000 acres of Stornoway Parish to the people, to be administered by the elected Stornoway Trust. His withdrawal from Lewis caused an economic slump, leading to the emigration of over 1000 able-bodied men to North America.

Leverburgh harbour, Harris; planned to be an industrial fishery town, but Lord Leverhulme's money ran out.

After the collapse of his schemes for Lewis, Leverhulme turned his attention to Harris, where the peaceful little village of Obbe was renamed Leverburgh and transformed into a bustling harbour town with all kinds of public works projects. But in May 1925 Lord Leverhulme died, and all developments stopped. Instead of becoming a town with a projected population of 10,000, Leverburgh reverted to being a sleepy village.

The economy of Harris is based on crofting and fishing, supplemented by income from tourism and from the district's most famous export, Harris Tweed. Originally a domestic activity, carried on mainly by women, the weaving of tweed became a full-time specialist male occupation, partly because the flying shuttle in 'modern' looms made the work heavier. In 1909 the Board of Trade approved a trade mark defining Harris Tweed as 'tweed, hand-spun, hand-woven and dyed and finished by hand in the Outer Hebrides', with 'made in Harris' or 'made in Lewis' added as appropriate. A Harris Tweed Association was formed and the distinctive orb surmounted by a cross has been in use since 1911. Today the industry is subject to the vagaries of the fashion industry, but in general clothes made from Harris Tweed are highly regarded, and priced appropriately. In recent years the amount produced has contracted, as market forces dictate that what was once a common and serviceable cloth is now a luxury item, but the islanders have proved adaptable in meeting this crisis. Some even produce tweed in the old way, hand-dyeing and carding, spinning on the wheel, hand-weaving and finishing, producing high-quality cloth selling for up to three times the price of ordinary tweed.

Just off the shore of North Harris, on the west coast, opposite the township of Hushinish, is the small rocky island of Scarp, rising to a height of 1011 feet (308m) on its north side. First settled in 1810, it was abandoned in 1971. In 1884 the population was estimated at around 200. As late as the 1940s the population was over 100; now the crofter's cottages are used as holiday homes and there are periodic threats to develop the island as a luxury holiday resort. Scarp was the scene of a strange experiment in 1934, when the German rocket scientist Gerhardt Zucher tried to persuade the British government that rockets could be used to transport mail and emergency medicines to remote islands. Amid much publicity, 30,000 letters were launched into the Hebridean air. But the rocket blew up and this attempt to use modern technology to solve the perennial problem of communication with remote communities was not repeated.

Until recently, the most remote community in Harris was Rhenigidale, accessible only by sea or by a rough hill track. But after lengthy representations a road was built, probably just in time to save this community from abandonment. There is a Gatcliffe Trust Hostel in the village.

Scalpay

Calmac ferries: Kyles Scalpay-Scalpay; passage time, 10 minutes.
Ferry information: Frequent sailings, vehicle booking not required.
No Sunday service.
Local ferry office: contact Caledonian MacBrayne Ltd, The Ferry
Terminal, Tarbert, Harris. Tel: (0859) 2444, Fax: (0859) 2017.

Railhead: Kyle of Lochalsh; ferry to Kyleakin, by road to Uig
(Skye), ferry to Tarbert (Harris).
Airport: none.
Accommodation: self-catering, limited B & B.
Tourist Information Centre: Pier Road, Tarbert, Harris. Tel: (0859)
2011.

The island of Scalpay (Norse: *skalp-r ay*, 'the island shaped like a boat') lies in the Outer Hebrides, just off the south-east corner of Harris, at the entrance to East Loch Tarbert. Access is by a small vehicular ferry from Kyles Scalpay on Harris, five miles (8km) east of Tarbert. Although only two square miles (5sq km) in size, the population is about 450, a small but tightly-knit community with a deserved reputation for innovation and enterprise. Its fishing fleet has been modernised, with the result that during the fishing industry's recent difficulties Scalpachs have maintained their island as a lively and viable community. In 1861 the population was 388, including some families evicted from the island of Pabbay in the Sound of Harris; by 1921 it had peaked at 624.

On the south-east corner of Scalpay is Eilean Glas lighthouse, now automatic. Its predecessor was one of the four original lighthouses built by the Commissioners of Northern Lights in 1789. The keepers' cottages are now holiday houses.

In December 1962 six Scalpay men went out in a small open boat in a gale to rescue the crew of the trawler *Boston Heron*; their consummate seamanship and bravery was recognised by the RNLI.

North Uist

Calmac ferries: Uig (Skye)-Lochmaddy; passage time, 3 hours 45 minutes. Tarbert (Harris)-Lochmaddy; passage time 1 hour 45 minutes. Alternatively, Oban-Lochboisdale (S. Uist) then by road across causeways to N. Uist. A small passenger ferry connects Newton Ferry (Port na Long) to Berneray and Harris (Leverburgh).
Ferry information: For vehicle reservations contact Caledonian MacBrayne Ltd, The Ferry Terminal, Uig, Isle of Skye. Tel: (047 042) 219, Fax: (047 042) 387.
Local ferry office: The Pier, Lochmaddy, North Uist. Tel: (087 63) 337, Fax: (087 63) 412.

Railhead: Kyle of Lochalsh, from where Calmac ferry to Skye and bus to Uig.
Airport: Benbecula has daily flights to Glasgow Airport, operated by British Airways; flight time, 1 hour. Loganair operates flights to Barra and Stornoway.
Accommodation: Hotels, guest-houses, B & B, self-catering.
Tourist Information Office: The Pier, Lochmaddy, North Uist. Tel: (087 63) 321.

The island of North Uist lies in the Outer Hebrides, between Harris and Benbecula, with a land area of 118 square miles (302sq km) and a population of about 1500. The chief village is Lochmaddy, linked by ferry to Tarbert on Harris and Uig on Skye. Calmac operates a 'triangular' service – **enquire from them full details**. A causeway links North Uist to Benbecula, where there is an airport. The highest hill is Eaval (1138ft/347m), in the south-east corner of the island.

There is an RSPB reserve near Balranald, on the western side of North Uist. It takes in 1625 acres of varying habitats: rocky coast, sandy beaches and dunes, machair, marshland and freshwater lochs. In fact, the headland of Ard an Runair within the reserve is the most westerly point of the Outer Hebrides and an ideal place for bird watching, especially during the spring and autumn migrations. Manx shearwater pass at the rate of over 1000 per hour. Gannets, fulmars, skuas and storm petrels are also commonly seen. In all, 183 species of birds have been recorded on the reserve, of which about fifty nest each year. Balranald is

*A house near Lochmaddy, North Uist, the ferry port linked to
Tarbert, Harris and Uig in the Isle of Skye.*

Looking westwards near Balranald, North Uist, to the Heisker or Monach Islands, and the North Atlantic.

especially good for waders, such as redshank, dunlin, oyster-catcher and ringer plover. There are 300 pairs of lapwing, and a dozen pairs of corncrakes, with their distinctive rasping call.

North Uist is a Protestant island, in contrast to its southern neighbours, and as such has more in common with Harris, although the intervening Sound of Harris is too deep to be bridged easily with a causeway. A passenger ferry links Newtonferry in North Uist with Leverburgh in Harris.

The north and west coasts have attractive sandy bays backed by wide expanses of machair, ablaze with colour in spring and summer. The landscape is dotted with interesting archaeological sites of different periods, notably the Neolithic chambered cairn of Barpa Langass, between Clachan and Lochmaddy, the only chambered cairn in the Western Isles with an intact burial chamber, and an impressive monument, 25m in diameter and 4m high. Another cairn, at Clettraval, has been severely robbed but is of interest because it belongs to the Clyde type, and is thus unique in the Western Isles. It is possible to get quite close to this cairn by using the road to the small defence installation on the summit of the hill South Clettraval,

*Communications equipment for the Western Isles rocket range
bristles on the summit of South Clettraval, North Uist.*

from where there is a panoramic view.

On the western slopes of Blashaval (358ft/109m), in
the north-west of the island, are three bronze age standing
stones called Na Fir Bhreige, the false men, improbably
said to be the graves of three spies who were buried alive.
The Iron Age Dun an t-Siamain, on a small island in a loch
on the west side of Eaval, can be reached by a curved
causeway. Another site on an island in a loch is the broch
of Dun an Sticir, not far from Newtonferry.

In recent years archaeologists have explored Eilean
Domhnuill, a small crannog or man-made island in Loch
Olabhat, near Griminish. Usually regarded as Iron Age
with dates in the early centuries BC, this example has
foundations nearly 5000 years old, putting it back into the
Neolithic period, and making it possibly the oldest artificial
island in Europe. Connected to the shore of the loch by a
stone causeway, the site yielded up hundreds of sherds of
pottery and dozens of flint flakes, giving the experts a real
insight into life in ancient times.

From the road just west of Loch Olabhat can be seen a
small tower standing in the loch at Scolpaig – not a well-
preserved prehistoric site, but a 'folly', constructed for
famine relief. Apparently there *was* an Iron Age 'dun' on

the site, which was quarried to build the tower. This is also a good point for viewing and hopefully photographing the Monach Islands, eight miles off the coast.

During the centuries of Norse occupation, North Uist was farmed by colonists from Norway, who have left their mark on the landscape in the many Norse place-names. The name 'Uist' is from the Norse *i-vist*, an abode or 'in-dwelling'. There is an important but ruinous medieval church site at Teampull na Trionaid in the south-west of the island, near the township of Carinish, reputedly founded by Somerled's daughter Beathag early in the thirteenth century. There was a monastery and college here, where the sons of chiefs were sent to be educated.

By 1850 the population had increased to 5000, but evictions carried out with much acrimony and bloodshed took place under the direction of the landowner, Lord MacDonald of Sleat. There was a violent confrontation between crofters and police at Malaclete. Nearby is the excavated archaeological site of the Udal, a settlement site occupied from the bronze age until the nineteenth century. The economy of the island today is based on crofting and fishing (mainly for lobsters and crabs), tourism, scallop farming, knitwear and tweed, and the alginate factory at Sponish on Loch Maddy.

With a circular road and hilly interior, North Uist is perfect for hill-walking. There is a regular bus service round the island, and occasional post buses as well. Offshore from Sollas is the tidal island of Vallay, an interesting destination for an easy walk – but watch the tides! The larger of the two houses on Vallay was built by Erskine Beveridge, who conducted early archaeological surveys of the Outer Hebrides, Coll and Tiree.

BENBECULA

The island of Benbecula (Gaelic: *Beinn a'bhfaodhla*, 'mountain of the fords') lies between North and South Uist. Today a road causeway replacing the previous fords connects all these islands together. The north ford, linking Benbecula to North Uist, was opened by the Queen Mother

in 1960. Despite the island's name, its only hill is called
Rueval (409ft/125m). Benbecula is about eight miles
(12.8km) wide by five miles (8km) from north to south. The
native population of 1300 is divided more or less equally
between the Protestantism of North Uist and the Roman
Catholicism of South Uist. Gaelic survives as the language
of everyday life, though a high proportion of the place-
names are of Norse origin. An additional 500 Royal
Artillery army personnel and dependents are stationed at
their base at Balivanich, providing support for the missile
range on South Uist. The operation has expanded greatly
from its small beginnings in 1959. An RAF radar station
was established in 1972 new radars were constructed on
Clettraval, North Uist, in 1981, while the control building
and associated facilities are at East Camp, Balivanich. A
small Second World War airfield, staffed by RAF techni-
cians, links the island with Barra, Stornoway and Glasgow;
of course, the ferries from Lochmaddy on North Uist and
Lochboisdale on South Uist provide links to Harris, Skye
and Oban.

The underlying geology is Lewisian gneiss, the
coastline indented, and the land surface of the island a
maze of tiny lochans. From the summit of Rueval there is a
fine view of the whole island. Peat is exposed on the shore
at Borve, proof that the Outer Isles are slowly sinking into
the Atlantic along their western edge, though at an
extremely slow rate.

Benbecula's natural beauty is somewhat marred by the
military facilities, but economically the island has
benefited. The army's NAAFI supermarket is the only one
in Britain open to the general public.

There are several sites of archaeological interest in
Benbecula's watery landscape. An exceptionally well-
preserved chambered long cairn and a ruined passage grave
lie close together in the centre of the island, half a mile east
of the main road. Near the northern causeway are two
stone circles, at Gramisdale. Most of their stones have
fallen. There is a good example of an Iron Age dun on an
island in Loch Dun Mhurchaidh, near Knock Rolum
township, joined to the shore by a causeway. Super-
imposed on the ruins of the dun are the ruins of a seven-

teenth century township.

Bonnie Prince Charlie sailed over the sea to Skye from here with Flora MacDonald in 1746, disguised as Betty Burke, after hiding in a cave for two days. He came within an ace of being captured there by the forces of General John Campbell of Mamore. The island was held by Clan Ranald, whose ruined fourteenth century castle, occupied until 1625, is at Borve. Near their eighteenth century house at Nunton is a fourteenth century chapel. The MacDonalds of Clanranald owned Benbecula until 1839, when it was sold to Colonel Gordon of Cluny, along with Barra, South Uist and Eriskay. Clan Ranald took its name from Ranald, the second son of the first marriage of John, 1st Lord of the Isles, to Amie MacRuari.

South Uist

Calmac ferries: Oban-Lochboisdale; passage time 5 hours 15 minutes.
Most sailings are via Castlebay (Barra); passage time, 7 hours 30
minutes. A small passenger ferry connects Ludag to Eriskay and
Eoligarry (Barra). Contact Tourist Information Office, Lochboisdale,
for details.
Ferry information: For vehicle reservations contact Caledonian
MacBrayne Ltd, The South Pier, Oban, Argyll. Tel: (0631) 62285,
Fax: (0631) 66588.
Local ferry office: The Pier, Lochboisdale. Tel: (087 84) 288.

Railhead: Oban.
Airport: Benbecula has daily flights to Glasgow Airport, operated by
British Airways; flight time, 1 hour. Loganair has connecting flights
to Barra and Stornoway.
Accommodation: Hotels, guest-houses, B & B, self-catering.
Tourist Information Centre: The Pier, Lochboisdale. Tel: (087 84)
286.

The island of South Uist is the second largest island in
the Outer Hebrides, linked to Benbecula to the north
by a causeway. With a land area of 141 square miles, it has
a population of 2400, concentrated into a narrow strip on
the western side between 20 miles (32km) of virtually
unbroken beach and peaty moorland rising to a mountainous spine running down the eastern side of the island.
Beinn Mhor (2034ft/620m) and Hecla (1988ft/606m) are
the two highest hills, with fine views from their summits.
The underlying bedrock is Lewisian gneiss.

The Loch Druidibeg National Nature Reserve to the
north of Drimsdale provides an ideal habitat for many
species of waterfowl, including native greylag geese, which
breed here. The corncrake, increasingly rare on the
mainland, is common here. There is a large colony of mute
swans on Loch Bee, at the north end of South Uist.

The east coast is deeply indented by four sea lochs. At
the head of the most southerly of these is the main village
and ferry terminal, Lochboisdale, with a population of
over 300. It has a hotel, police station, post office, doctor,
dentist, garages, school, shops and the island's Tourist
Information Centre. There are ferry connections from

*A ruined croft in South Uist; emigration and depopulation is a
continuing problem in this fragile island community.*

One of Calmac's newest ferries, The Lord of the Isles, *approaching the pier at Lochboisdale, South Uist.*

Lochboisdale to Oban and Castlebay (Barra). From the south tip of South Uist there are passenger ferries to Eriskay and Barra.

At Daliburgh, two miles (3.2km) west of Lochboisdale, there is a hotel, post office, shops, school, petrol station, maternity hospital and old folks' home. To the south, the road goes six miles (9.6km) to Pollachar, where there is a picturesque early nineteenth century inn, and stupendous views across to Eriskay and Barra. Near the inn is a standing stone.

North of Daliburgh the main road runs up the west side of the island, with many side roads leading down to crofts and beaches. Of special interest is the road through Bornish to the shore at Rubha Ardvule, which has beautiful beaches, both freshwater and seashore habitats, and an Iron Age fort.

There are many sites of archaeological interest, including the excavated prehistoric aisled house at Kilpheder and the Reinaval passage grave on the northern shoulder of the hill just south of the township of Mingary. Dun Mor is an iron age fortified island in a loch just south of the township of West Gerinish, while Dun Uiselan is a similar site in another loch, west of the township of Ollag.

Beinn a'Charra Bronze Age standing stone, South Uist, overlooking the crofting townships of Staoinebrig and Ormacleit.

Two churches at Howmore, dedicated to St Mary and St Columba, may date from Early Christian times, perhaps as early as the seventh century. The graveyard at Hallan contains one of the few sixteenth century carved grave slabs to be found in the Western Isles.

Just north of Milton, a cairn marks the birthplace of Flora MacDonald, who helped Bonnie Prince Charlie evade capture and assisted his escape. Disguised as her maid 'Betty Burke', they sailed to Skye from Benbecula in a small boat on 28 June 1746. The island suffered badly from clearances in the nineteenth century, as a result of the policies of Colonel Gordon of Cluny, who bought it, along with the neighbouring islands of Benbecula and Eriskay, from the MacDonalds of Clanranald in 1838. Between 1841 and 1861 the population fell from 7300 to 5300, as townships were cleared for sheep. Many emigrated to North America.

South Uist's economy is dominated by the army missile range on the north-west corner of the island, from where rockets are fired out over the Atlantic, their progress monitored by a tracking station on St Kilda. Other sources of income are crofting, fishing (mainly for lobsters and crabs), shellfish farming, and seaweed processing. The

*Houses near Lochboisdale, South Uist, Calmac's ferry terminal
connecting with Castlebay in Barra and Oban on the Scottish
mainland.*

*A ruined croft near Lochboisdale; on the south part of South Uist
there are many similarly sad homes.*

missile range control installation, known locally as 'space city', dominates the skyline of Rueval, and dwarfs the 30 foot (9m) granite statue of 'Our Lady of the Isles' by Hew Lorimer (1959). It is possible to drive right to the top of this hill, where, turning one's back on the communications' 'golfballs', there are spectacular panoramic views. In clear weather St Kilda is visible to the west.

This mainly Roman Catholic island with its many roadside shrines has a more relaxed attitude to Sabbatarianism than the Protestant islands to the north.

ERISKAY

The island of Eriskay (Norse: *Eiriks-ey*, 'Eric's island') lies in the Outer Hebrides between South Uist and Barra. A local ferry boat, the *Eilean na h-Oige* suggests an alternative Gaelic meaning, 'the Isle of Youth'. Only 2.5 by 1.5 miles (4 by 2.5 km) in size, Eriskay is the mostly densely populated Hebridean island with a population of 200. The economy of the mainly Roman Catholic community is based on an enterprising fishing industry, supplemented by crofting and hand-knitted woolly jumpers. There are ferry connections to South Uist and Barra.

Ben Scrien (610ft/186m) is the highest hill, overlooking the township of Balla, with a shop, school, post office and church.

Bonnie Prince Charlie first landed on Scottish soil at Eriskay in 1745. The beach where he stepped ashore is called *Coilleag a'Phrionnsa*, where a small pink convolvolus reputedly but inaccurately said to be found nowhere else in the world flowers in July. The 'Eriskay Love Lilt' is a famous Gaelic folk song. In 1941 the merchant ship *Politician*, carrying 20,000 cases of whisky, foundered off Eriskay. Five thousand cases were salvaged locally and unofficially, the basis of Sir Compton MacKenzie's novel *Whisky Galore!*; an Ealing comedy film was made in Barra in 1948. In 1991 the islanders expect an influx of journalists, camera crews and sightseers, as salvage operations on the wreck continue and its fiftieth anniversary is celebrated. As well as 24,000 cases of whisky the ship was also carrying

*A typical Hebridean beach, on the island of Eriskay, reached by
passenger ferry from Ludag jetty, South Uist.*

The Lord of the Isles *loading at Oban; many island piers have recently been modernised to accommodate the new roll-on roll-off ferries.*

The Isle of Mull *in Oban Bay, with Kerrara and the mountains of Mull in the background; it normally serves both Mull and Colonsay.*

some £3 million in Jamaican currency. The local pub opened in 1988, an ugly modern building but a very welcome addition to the island's facilities. It is called, unsurprisingly, 'Am Politician', and has a small collection of photographs and memorabilia.

The island's small Catholic church, St Michael's, is worth a visit. Opened in 1903, it owes its existence to Father Allan MacDonald, a well-known folklorist and collector of Gaelic stories and songs. The design is based on churches he saw in Spain during his training at Valladolid. The church bell comes from the German battleship *Derfflinger*, scuttled at Scapa Flow in Orkney at the end of the First World War. The altar is the bow of a lifeboat from the aircraft carrier *Hermes*, washed ashore on Eriskay after being lost on an exercise off St Kilda.

Eriskay ponies are the last survivors of the native Scottish pony, and are the subject of a conservation breeding scheme. They stand 12–13 hands high, with small ears and are still used to carry peat and seaweed.

*Kisimull Castle, from which Castlebay in Barra takes its name, for a
thousand years the fortress home of the MacNeills of Barra.*

*The Post Office, Castlebay, Barra – a busy place when the ferry is
about to depart for Oban.*

Barra

Calmac ferries: Oban-Castlebay; passage time, 5 hours. Lochboisdale
(South Uist)-Castlebay; passage time 1 hour 45 minutes.
A small passenger ferry connects Eoligary (Barra) to Ludag (S. Uist).
Ferry information: For vehicle reservations contact Caledonian
MacBrayne Ltd, the South Pier, Oban, Argyll. Tel: (0631) 62285,
Fax: (0631) 66588. The Sunday service formerly operating Mallaig-
Castlebay no longer runs.

Railhead: Oban
Airport: Northbay, Barra. Daily service to Glasgow Airport,
operated by Loganair; flight time, 65 minutes. Also flights to
Benbecula and Stornoway.
Car and bicycle hire: Castlebay.
Island newspaper: *Guth Bharraidh* (the Voice of Barra).
Accommodation: Hotels, guest-houses, self-catering, B & B,
caravans, camping.
Tourist Information Centre: Main Street, Castlebay, Isle of Barra,
Tel: (087 14) 336.

B arra is an island at the southern end of the Outer
Hebrides, separated from South Uist by the Sound of
Barra and the island of Eriskay. Only eight miles (12.8km)
from north to south and between four and five miles
(6.4–8km) wide, it supports a population of about 1200 on
its 20 square miles (51sq km). About 12 miles (19km) of
road encircle the island, with a northern spur to the airport
at Traigh Mhor and the jetty at Eoligarry.

The island takes its name from St Barr (Finbarr); the
church of Cille Bharra near Northbay airport dates from
the twelfth century. It was the parish for the island in the
Middle Ages. Inside are carved grave-slabs and a small
display explaining the history of the church, including the
famous Runic Stone, which has Norse runes on one side
and a Christian cross on the other. The runes have been
translated as: 'This cross has been raised in memory of
Thorgeth, daughter of Steinar'. Sir Compton MacKenzie is
buried in the graveyard.

There are several ancient sites on Barra: cairns,
standing stones, and forts. The broch at Dun Cuier,
Allasdale, has been excavated. Barra has always been a

*Loganair plane at Barra Airport on the cockle strand, Traigh Mor,
Barra; the timetable varies according to the tide!*

Reflections near Bruernish, North Bay, Barra, with a statue of St Barr; his church at Cille Bharra is medieval.

Castlebay, Barra, the main town and administrative centre of a
relatively prosperous and predominantly Roman Catholic island.

fertile island, and was an attractive proposition in prehistoric times. Even today it has an air of tidiness and prosperity missing from its northern neighbours.

On the west side of the island are miles of sandy beaches, backed by machair land which bursts into colour with a carpet of wild flowers in May and June. At one end of the wide sands of Hallaman beach is the modernistic and controversial Isle of Barra Hotel. The east coast is rockier, with more dramatic coastal scenery. Inland the land is rocky, and covered with heather and peat.

The main village is Castlebay, linked to Oban and Lochboisdale on South Uist by car ferry. It takes its name from the picturesque and much-photographed Kisimull castle, the ancestral stronghold of the MacNeills of Barra from 1427, when they received a charter from Alexander, Lord of the Isles, confirmed by James IV in 1495. When sold for debt to Colonel Gordon of Cluny in 1838, the island was offered to the government as a penal colony. Clearances later in the nineteenth century led to massive emigration.

Kisimull castle, dating from the eleventh century, consists of a square keep within a curtain wall, which is shaped to fit the contours of the islet on which it stands. It

is similar in design to other early castles in the west of
Scotland, such as Dunstaffnage, Castle Tioram, Mingarry
and Breachacha (Coll). It was bought in 1937, along with
12,000 acres (4860 hectares) of land, by the 45th MacNeil
of Barra, an American architect, who restored it to its
present state before his death in 1970. According to clan
tradition, a retainer used to announce daily from the castle
walls 'MacNeil has dined, the Kings, Princes and others of
the earth may now dine'. There are boat trips to the castle
from the pier at Castlebay.

Castlebay provides a full range of services: shops,
doctor, church, bank, post office, secondary school, library
and accommodation. High on the hill above the town is a
massive statue of the Virgin Mary with the infant Jesus,
erected in 1954 to mark the Roman Catholic Church's
Marian year. The marble statue, made in Italy, was carried
up the mountain by relays of twelve men. From the summit
of Heaval (1260ft/384m) there are magnificent views to
north and south.

Gaelic culture is strong and healthy in Barra, sustained
by the Church and by a rich store of folklore and song.
Barra has a reputation as a place which knows how to
enjoy itself, and with its Catholic tradition is unhindered
by Sabbatarianism. The church in Castlebay, Our Lady,
Star of the Sea, was built in 1889.

Castlebay was once the site of a thriving herring
industry, but now supports only a small-scale commercial
fishery catching mainly white fish, prawns and lobsters.
Most islanders are crofter-fishermen, keeping sheep and
cattle and growing a few vegetables, especially potatoes.
Tourism is increasingly important. There are several craft
shops on the island, and a perfume factory, at Tangusdale.

There is a daily air service to Glasgow the airstrip is on
the beach at Traigh Mhor, at the north end of the island,
the only one in the United Kingdom where schedules are
shown as 'subject to tides'. The air service to Barra was
started by Northern and Scottish Airways Ltd in 1936, and
since 1975 has been operated by Loganair. Landings are
not possible within three hours either side of high tide.

Barra was the location for the famous Ealing comedy
film *Whisky Galore!*, made in 1948, and based on

Compton MacKenzie's novel. It gives a very amusing and only slightly exaggerated account of events on the neighbouring island of Eriskay, where the 12,000 ton SS *Politician*, carrying 250,000 bottles of whisky, was wrecked in 1941. Many of Barra's older residents were extras in the film, which is the subject of documentaries celebrating the fiftieth anniversary of the wreck.

VATERSAY

The island of Vatersay, to the south of Barra, can now be reached by a 250 yard (229m) long causeway opened in 1990, at a cost of 4 million, including a new road over the hill from Castlebay. Over 200,000 tonnes of rock were blasted for this project, which the islanders view as a lifesaver for their small community. Vatersay is three square miles in area with a Gaelic-speaking population of around seventy.

In 1908 the Vatersay Raiders were imprisoned for occupying some of the island's fertile land. They were from Barra and Uist, starved for land. In 1911 there were 288 people on this tiny island, including many immigrants from Barra and Mingulay. The present crofts, shop, post office, church, school and village hall are scattered round the island's five miles (8km) of road. The highest point is Heishival Mor (625ft/191m); to the south are The Bishop's Isles and Mingulay, all now uninhabited. It is sometimes possible to organise boat trips to these islands – enquire locally or at the Tourist Information Centre in Barra.

Index